EDITOR: I

OSPREY
MILITARY

ELITE

2

AMERICAN
ZOUAVES

Text by
ROBIN SMITH
Colour plates by
BILL YOUNGHUSBAND

Filmset in Great Britain by KDI, Newton le Willows
Printed through World Print Ltd, Hong Kong

FOR A CATALOGUE OF ALL BOOKS PUBLISHED BY OSPREY
MILITARY, AUTOMOTIVE AND AVIATION PLEASE WRITE TO:

The Marketing Manager, Osprey Publishing, PO Box 140,
Wellingborough, Northants, NN8 4ZA, United Kingdom

or visit Osprey's website at:
http://www.osprey-publishing.co.uk

Acknowledgments

The author would like to thank the following gentlemen for
their help in preparing this book. The roll of honour reads:
Ron Field, Brian Pohanka, Mike McAfee, Martin L.
Schoenfeld, Martin Windrow, Richard Warren, Tim Newark,
Richard O'Sullivan, Paul Smith, Martin Gladstone, John
Madge, Bill Torrens, Jim Samuelson, John Robinson, Dave
Boaz, Pat Schroeder and all my comrades in the recreated 5th
New York. Three huzzahs and a tiger for you all.
This book is for Peter Smith. Remember the Alamo.

Publisher's note

Readers may wish to study this title in conjunction with the
following Osprey publications:

MAA 177 *American Civil War Armies (2): Union*
MAA 38 *Army of the Potomac*
MAA 258 *Flags of the American Civil War (2): Union*
MAA 265 *Flags of the American Civil War (3): State and
         Volunteer*
MAA 168 *US Cavalry 1850–90*
Warrior 13 *Union Cavalryman 1861–1865*
Campaign 10 *First Bull Run 1861*
Campaign 17 *Chickamauga*
Campaign 32 *Antietam 1862*

Artist's note

Readers may care to note that the original paintings from
which the colour plates in this book were prepared are
available for private sale. All reproduction copyright what-
soever is retained by the Publishers. All enquiries should be
addressed to:

William Younghusband
12 St Andrew's Walk
Chapel Allerton
Leeds LS7 3PS

The Publishers regret that they can enter into no corre-
spondence upon this matter.

INTRODUCTION

Storming the heights of the Alma, charging gallantly at Inkerman and scrambling up the Malakoff at Sebastopol during the Crimean War, the elite Zouaves of the French Army became the subject of many heroic paintings and illustrations. Across Europe and America their daring reputation caught the imagination. Queen Victoria even had one of her colonial regiments, the West India Regiment, wear Zouave dress.

General George B. McClellan, who as a captain had been an American observer in the Crimea, called French Zouaves the 'beau-ideal of a soldier', and many Union volunteers, and some Confederates, fancied themselves as brave 'Zoos-Zoos'. During the course of the American Civil War more than 50 Zouave regiments were formed, mostly in the North.

One New York Zouave regiment was composed largely of French immigrants, while others had sprinklings of French personnel. But like many regiments in the American Civil War, these exotic units boasted an array of nationalities in their ranks, including British, Germans, Swedes, Italians and Irishmen – all attracted by the glamour of being a Zouave.

American Zouave regiments based themselves on the fine reputation that had been built up by the French Zouaves. The original Zouaves had

This period print shows a scene in the Crimean War when the Zouaves led a spectacular charge and came to the aid of the British Guards, hard pressed on the right flank at Inkerman. 'Their trumpets sounded above the din of battle and when we watched their eager advance on the flank of the enemy we knew the day was won,' wrote William Howard Russell, correspondent for the London Times. *Russell also covered the American Civil War and was complimentary about the Louisiana Zouaves he saw. (Author's collection)*

A dashing Zouave adorns the cover of this music score, sharing the stage with a couple of Italian Bersaglieri. The public was bombarded with Zouave images throughout the 19th century, and the American Civil War would be the perfect opportunity for many volunteers to try and emulate their exploits. (Author's collection)

been natives of the Zouaoua tribe mixed with some French settlers, who had served with the French Army during France's North African campaigns in the 1830s. Their native North African dress – baggy trousers, short jacket and fez – became the basis of the famous Zouave uniform that remained virtually unchanged for more than 50 years; at the beginning of the First World War French Zouaves marched to the front in uniforms little different to those worn in the Crimea. The French originally raised two battalions of native Zouaves; but by the time of the Crimean War, three Zouave regiments of the line had been created entirely from Frenchmen, and a regiment of Imperial Guard Zouaves was raised in 1855. The appeal of being a Zouave was so great that non-commissioned officers often gave up their stripes to serve as privates in these regiments. The Zouaves saw hard service in the Crimea, where they had a great affinity with the wild

Highlanders of the British Army. In 1859, during the Italian campaign, when France joined in the fight against the Austrians for Italy's independence, the 3rd Zouaves won a gold medal for their conduct at Palestro, and all their officers were decorated with the Military Order of Savoy.

Four years later, while their American brothers-in-arms were fighting for the North and South, French Zouaves saw much action in the 'Mexican Adventure', adding the honours Puebla and San-Lorenzo to their achievements. American Zouaves had a formidable reputation to live up to. Most succeeded; some failed, but all considered themselves to be an elite.

THE AMERICAN ZOUAVE CRAZE

Gunned down at the beginning of the American Civil War, Elmer E. Ellsworth never even tasted battle, but he sparked a Zouave craze across America. Born in the village of Malta near Mechanicville, New York State, on 11 April 1837, Ellsworth became a military enthusiast at an early age, putting his friends armed with sticks through drill movements in the schoolyard. When he moved to New York City, Ellsworth frequently visited the drill sessions of the 'Dandy Seventh', the 7th Regiment, New York State Militia, a crack unit who were also nicknamed the 'Old Greybacks' because of their grey uniforms. Later, as a struggling law student in Chicago, Ellsworth met up with Charles A. DeVilliers, a former French Army surgeon who had served with a Zouave regiment in the Crimea.

Ellsworth's imagination was fired, and he formed his own Zouave unit, proudly named the United States Zouave Cadets, from a company of the Illinois State Militia. Ellsworth issued a challenge to any volunteer or regular regiment in the United States to take on his men in a drill competition, but no other outfits took up the challenge.

Instead, in 1860 Ellsworth took his cadets on a drill display tour of 19 East Coast cities. The public loved the Zouave Cadets, and Ellsworth became a celebrity: his portrait sold by the thousand, and ladies swooned over the dashing young officer and his men. The Old Greybacks, whom Ellsworth had lovingly watched in his youth, freely admitted that no other unit could touch the Zouave Cadets for their precision; at the call of a bugle, Ellsworth's men performed gymnastic drill movements, including square, triangle and double cross formations.

Newspapers were full of stories about Zouave exploits. 'A Zouave is a fellow who can climb a greased pole feet first, carrying a barrel of pork in his teeth – that is a Zouave,' ran one enthusiastic account in a Chicago newspaper. 'A fellow who can take a five shooting revolver in each hand and knock the spots out of the ten of diamonds at 80 paces, turning somersaults all the time and firing every shot in the air – that is a Zouave.

Ellsworth and his men had established a Zouave craze in America, but maintaining the crack unit proved too expensive, and the Zouave Cadets were eventually disbanded. Ellsworth moved to Springfield, Illinois, entered Abraham Lincoln's law office and campaigned on the future president's behalf. He was invited by Lincoln to

These French Zouaves on exercise around 1913 wear uniforms that wouldn't have been out of place in the Crimean War. French Zouaves wore their traditional uniforms during the first months of World War I, but sustained such heavy casualties that they were ordered to wear less conspicuous dress. (Author's collection)

The United States Zouave Cadets run through their display in New York in 1860. Captain Ellsworth, their founder, is the officer with drawn sword at the right of the picture. Part drill and part gymnastics, the displays given by the Cadets were military theatre on a grand scale, lapped up by crowds everywhere. In the audience in New York was Colonel Abram Duryée, who was impressed by the display and went on to found the famed 5th New York Volunteer Infantry, Duryée's Zouaves. (Michael J McAfee)

THE CHICAGO ZOUAVES EXECUTING THEIR DRILL IN NEW YORK, JULY, 1860.—[FROM A PHOTOGRAPH BY GURNEY.]

This engraving shows the Fire Zouaves in their distinctive grey uniforms marching down Broadway and off to the war. The Zouaves were the pride of New York in the heady days of 1861, but the solid citizens of Washington, where the Fire Zouaves were first stationed, didn't take kindly to their wild antics.(Brian Pohanka)

accompany him to Washington, and he saw this as a chance to enter the War Office and start a National Militia Bureau in the Federal Government, with himself at the head. But, his dream was never realised.

FIREMEN ZOUAVES

Early in 1861, Ellsworth was commissioned a second lieutenant in the regular army, but he resigned this post shortly after the firing on Fort Sumter and the beginning of war. He headed back to New York with the romantic idea that his native state should supply the first Zouave unit to go to Washington and be mustered in for the conflict.

Ellsworth had been a martinet with his Zouave Cadets: his men had to be of sound moral character and they were not allowed to drink (ideas that would have appalled roguish French Zouaves, whose speciality in the Crimea had been plundering broken-down supply carts laden with food and liquor). For his new regiment, the 11th New York Volunteer Infantry, Ellsworth's First

New York Fire Zouaves, Ellsworth turned to the tough firemen of New York City for recruits. 'I want the New York firemen for there are no more effective men in the country and none with whom I can do so much,' he said.

The firemen agreed with him and recruiting went splendidly. Within 48 hours the muster rolls of the 11th New York were full. The Fire Zouaves arrived in Washington on 7 May 1861, spoiling for a fight. Many of them had their heads shaved, and some even sported patriotic emblems, such as eagles, carved into the stubble.

The regiment was quartered in the Capitol's House of Representatives, and the men amused themselves by swinging on ropes from the unfinished Rotunda's cornice and hanging like monkeys from the edge of the dome. Hungry Fire Zouaves seized a stray pig and cut its throat, while other members in boisterous mood bought some shoes at a bootmaker's and asked for the bill to be sent to President Lincoln.

The Zouaves also stole a fire engine, towing it triumphantly around town, and they set fire to an effigy of Confederate president Jeff Davis suspended from a tree, starting rumours that they had hanged and burned an innocent passer-by.

Ellsworth dressed his men down, and they redeemed themselves by putting out a fire at a

Jackson, the owner of the building, shot Ellsworth dead. Jackson was in turn fatally shot by Fire Zouave corporal Francis E. Brownell, who had followed Ellsworth into the building.

The Fire Zouaves threatened to torch Alexandria, and the news that the dashing young Zouave commander was dead devastated

Despite their brief career, the Fire Zouaves carried no fewer than five colours, displayed in this period **Harper's Weekly Illustration.** *The most well known is the colour second left. Beautifully illustrated with firemen's equipment, this colour was given to the Zouaves by the New York Fire Department. The original regimental colour of the Fire Zouaves was presented by Mrs John J. Astor and embroidered with the words 'US National Guards, First Regiment Zouaves New York'. (Ron Field)*

tailor's shop next to the famous Willard's Hotel. Grateful citizens had a collection for the daring Zouaves and the Willard's Hotel proprietor presented the regiment with 500 dollars.

On the night of 23 May 1861 the regiment moved out of Washington and crossed into Virginia, taking part in an action to seize Alexandria, a Confederate-held town in the pre-dawn hours of 24 May. Incensed at seeing a Confederate flag flying from the Marshall House, a tavern in Alexandria, Ellsworth impulsively rushed into the building, marched upstairs and tore the flag down. As he came downstairs, James

Few men who have never seen a battle can have had such a profound effect on military thinking as Elmer E. Ellsworth. This picture of the gallant commander of the United States Zouave Cadets, the flashy outfit who did so much to popularise Zouaves in America, was taken in New York in 1860 while the Cadets were on tour. The former struggling law student looks every inch a gallant soldier – and we can only wonder what he would have achieved during the civil war, if his life hadn't been ended by a shotgun toting tavern owner, shortly after the outbreak of hostilities. (Michael J. McAfee)

This tough-looking character is Corporal Francis E. Brownell, the Fire Zouave who gunned down Colonel Ellsworth's killer, James Jackson, in an Alexandria tavern. This photo may have been taken before the incident, though, as later photos show Brownell wearing a black armband in mourning for his dead commander. Just visible under Brownell's jacket is his belt bearing the word 'Premier', the fire company Brownell served with before the war. (Michael J. McAfee)

was commissioned a lieutenant in the regular army and was later awarded the Congressional Medal of Honour for shooting Ellsworth's killer down. After Ellsworth's demise Noah L. Farnham, the 11th New York's lieutenant colonel, assumed command of the Fire Zouaves. Serving with the 7th Regiment New York State Militia, Farnham became Ellsworth's close friend after watching the United States Zouave Cadets in action. Just before his death, when the 7th and the Fire Zouaves were posted to Washington, Ellsworth had offered Farnham a command with his unit.

Lieutenant Colonel Noah Farnham, the second commander of the Fire Zouaves, walked arm in arm with Ellsworth when the regiment left New York, but here he wears a black armband after his comrade's demise. Farnham wears a grey Fire Zouaves officer's frock coat, embellished with gold trim on the cuffs. He was mortally wounded at First Bull Run, but won praise for his conduct during the battle. (Michael J. McAfee)

Washington. Flags were lowered to half mast and Ellsworth's body lay in state at the engine house in the Washington Navy Yard. Ellsworth had been a favourite of President Lincoln, and his funeral service was held in the East Room of the White House. Hundreds of mourners filed past his coffin to gaze at the gallant colonel, dressed in his uniform with white lilies pinned to his frock coat. Songs were written in his honour, and he became a martyr for the Union cause. Corporal Brownell

Farnham led the dispirited Fire Zouaves into their baptism of fire at the Battle of First Bull Run in July 1861. With a battalion of Marines, they were ordered to give support to two Union artillery batteries getting into position on Henry House Hill, ready to open up on the rebel line. The Zouaves and the Marines were crossing the crest of the hill when the batteries came under fierce Confederate fire. Nearly every cannoneer was cut down, and the unnerved Zouaves and Marines broke and ran. It wasn't complete panic though: some Zouaves made a stand, firing over the heads of their retreating comrades.

Colonel Farnham and his staff tried to rally the regiment, but at the height of the action Farnham's horse was shot out from under him and he was struck a glancing blow on the head by a bullet. From a screening line of woods to the right of the Union position the famed 1st Virginia Cavalry, led by the dashing Jeb Stuart, saw an opportunity and charged the mass of Zouaves.

The 11th New York were unaware of the cavalry until they were nearly upon them, and again they ran. However, Stuart's cavalry did little damage, and several were unhorsed by Zouave bayonets. Carried from the field, Colonel Farnham seemed to make a recovery from his wounds, but on 14 August, a few weeks after Bull Run, he died.

As untested troops, the Fire Zouaves did no better or worse than many regiments at First Bull Run, and if Ellsworth had been with them it might have been a different story. However, they did win some praise. Colonel O.B. Wilcox of the 1st Michigan Infantry wrote: 'The Zouaves, though broken as a regiment, did good service under my own eyes in the woods, and detachments of them joined other regiments in the fight.' Farnham and his staff were also singled out for compliments, but after First Bull Run the Fire Zouaves would never have the opportunity to prove themselves; some months later the regiment was disbanded.

NEW YORK'S FINEST

Duryée's Zouaves

A few weeks before the demise of the Fire Zouaves the 5th New York Volunteer Infantry, Duryée's Zouaves, had proved their mettle with a charge at Big Bethel, the first land action of the American Civil War, and throughout its two-year service the 5th would live up to all its ideals. The unit would also hold the grim record that in the entire war no other Union infantry regiment suffered so great a number of casualties in so short a space of time, during a single day's battle.

Mustered in on 22 April 1861, the 5th New York Volunteer Infantry was commanded by Colonel Abram Duryée, elected to the post by a

The 5th New York march down Broadway on their way to war in 1861. This woodcut, based on a sketch by the artist and reporter Frank Vizetelly, was featured in the London Illustrated News *on 22 June 1861. Note the band, who appear to be wearing some kind of fezzes with visors on the fronts. This is probably artistic licence. (Brian Pohanka)*

group of military enthusiasts meeting in Manhattan to organise a new volunteer regiment. Originally called the Advance Guard, the regiment soon became better known as Duryée's Zouaves.

Abram Duryée was a wealthy mahogany merchant and former commanding officer of the famed 7th New York, where he had built up a fine reputation as a drillmaster. Duryée had seen a display by Ellsworth's Zouave Cadets and decided that his new regiment would be Zouaves. The 5th New York quickly achieved an elite status, boasting a high proportion of well-educated men. Recruited largely in Manhattan, 80 per cent of the regiment were native-born Americans, but it also boasted dozens of Englishmen in its ranks. At the Battle of Second Bull Run, the 5th's costliest engagement, both the regiment's British-born colour bearers, Sergeant Andrew B. Allison and Sergeant Francis Spelman, were mortally wounded.

On 23 May 1861 the 5th New York proudly marched off to war, 848 strong; when the regiment returned home two years later, fewer than 300 men were left in the ranks. The regiment's baptism of fire, at Big Bethel in

5th New York officers on the steps of the Segar House near Camp Hamilton, Virginia, 1861. Lieutenant Colonel Gouverneur Kemble Warren flourishes a telescope, while the gentleman at the front striking a memorable pose is Colonel Duryée. Regimental chaplain Gordon Winslow is seated at the table, and adjutant Hamblin is the tall man standing in the background wearing a kepi. (Brian Pohanka)

Virginia on 10 June 1861, came when Union forces attempted to capture a Confederate encampment. Singing 'Bingo', a popular song of the time, the 5th New York charged proudly into battle, attacking in a thickly wooded area heavily under fire from Confederate artillery.

Part of Colonel Duryée's uniform was torn away at the shoulder, while Captain Judson Kilpatrick, the commander of Company H, was badly cut through the thigh by canister shot. Kilpatrick, who became a cavalry commander later in the war and was nicknamed 'Kill Cavalry' because of the way he drove his men, continued to stagger forward, until the pain of his wound forced him to give up.

But such gallantry was wasted: after a couple of hours the Federals had failed to capture the encampment and gave up their assault. The fight had cost the 5th New York six dead and 13 wounded.

In July 1861 the 5th New York were ordered to Baltimore, Maryland, for an eight-month stint of garrison duty. Maryland was a state with much pro-Southern sympathy, and some sections of the community did not take kindly to the regiment, but gentlemen all, Duryée's Zouaves became popular in Baltimore. Several of them even married local belles, who were left behind in

March 1862, when the 5th New York joined the Union assault on Richmond up through the Virginia Peninsula; there they were brigaded with the regular troops of General George Sykes' division.

At Gaines' Mill on 27 June, one of the Seven Days Battles to stop the Federals threatening Richmond, the 5th New York was involved in a series of desperate charges against superior rebel forces, smashing into the 1st South Carolina Rifles no fewer than three times. During the battle the 5th's two colour bearers stood 30 paces in front of the regiment's line and defied the enemy. Inspired by this action, the 5th went in with the bayonet, but despite such courage the Confederate line held.

Exhausted and out of ammunition, the 5th was relieved by the 1st Pennsylvania Reserves. With shells exploding all around his Zouaves, Lieutenant Colonel Hiram Duryea, the regiment's third commander, coolly ordered the 5th into line and had them count off. Despite their hard fight, he wanted the ranks dressed properly before the men marched off to replenish their cartridge boxes.

Earlier in the battle Duryea had been cheered by his men as he calmly trotted up and down the 5th's line on his horse, Black Jack, not even

flinching when a shell ploughed into the ground right under the animal. The 5th's bloodiest day came at Second Bull Run in August 1862. Brigaded with the 10th New York, they were hit by a huge Confederate attack from Longstreet's Corps. Bludgeoned from three sides at once, 120 members of the 5th New York were killed or mortally wounded in seven minutes, 179 were wounded and 27 were captured. Out of a total of 550 men, 326 were casualties. In the entire war, no other Union infantry regiment lost as many men in such a short space of time – during a single day's battle.

Many of the wounded Zouaves had been hit more than once, and even those who survived the carnage had bullet holes through their clothes and were badly scratched. Sergeant Andrew B. Allison, who carried the national colours, was shot through the wrist and then through the heart. Regimental colour bearer Sergeant Francis Spelman had multiple wounds but clung grimly to his standard, yelling: 'For God's sake don't let them take my flag.' Spelman died a few days after the battle; despite the carnage, the 5th's colours were borne to safety as the remnants of the Zouaves retreated, every man for himself.

Two Zouaves waded through a stream, and their baggy trousers filled up with water. Members of the 5th Texas took pot shots at the hapless New Yorkers, and some of their bullets pierced one of the Zouave's sodden trousers. Out squirted jets of water, and the rebels couldn't stop themselves laughing.

The 5th New York went on to serve at Antietam, Shepherdstown, Fredericksburg and Chancellorsville, but its casualties remained light.

Zouaves were front page news in 1861. This illustration from **Harper's Weekly** shows the 5th New York, Duryée's Zouaves, at Fortress Monroe in Virginia. The flowing pieces of cloth worn under their fezzes, also seen in the illustration of the 5th marching down Broadway, are called havelocks; popular items in the early Civil War years. At the start of the war, 5th New York Zouaves sometimes wore turbans around their fezzes and their havelocks buttoned up around their chins. (Ron Field)

After Chancellorsville, in May 1863, the regiment's term of service expired and the battle-hardened veterans of Duryée's Zouaves returned home, parading down Broadway. 'The men were brown and rugged; their colors were weather-stained and bullet-torn; their uniforms were tattered and stained with Virginia mud and the smoke of hard-fought conflicts. They looked magnificent,' reported the *New York Times*.

The reputation of Duryée's Zouaves didn't end with the regiment's homecoming parade. Two other regiments had their roots in the 5th: the 165th New York, also known as the Second Battalion Duryée Zouaves, and the 5th New York Veteran Volunteers. Men of the original 5th New York, who had signed on for three years and whose time of service had not expired, were transferred to the 146th New York.

165th New York
After Second Bull Run a detail of officers and men from the depleted ranks of the 5th were sent to New York to recruit for the regiment. The cash bounties they offered at the 5th's recruiting office in Manhattan and the good name of the regiment attracted so many recruits that a new eight-company battalion was raised, becoming the 165th New York. Commanded by Lieutenant-colonel Abel Smith Jnr, the regiment was quartered at Camp Washington, on Staten Island, where they were mustered in on 28 November 1862 and presented with their colours by a group of dignitaries on 13 December.

Plans to create a four-regiment Zouave brigade in the Army of the Potomac were shelved with the removal of General George McClellan from command, and the 165th were ordered down to Louisiana, where they joined General Nathaniel Banks' forces attacking Port Hudson, the Confederate stronghold on the Mississippi River.

On 27 May 1863 the 165th took part in a ferocious assault on the rebel defences. The cost was high: the 165th lost 108 Zouaves, more than a third of its men. Lieutenant-colonel Abel Smith was mortally wounded, and both colour bearers and five men of the colour guard were killed.

Major Felix Agnus took over command of the 165th New York. A Frenchman who had served

Corporal 5th New York, Federal Hill, Baltimore, autumn 1861. Note that he is wearing leather greaves, known as jambieres, above his gaiters and is armed with a Sharps rifle. Only Companies E and I of the 5th New York, who were used as skirmishers, were issued with these famous breech-loading rifles. (Richard Tibbals)

with the French 3rd Regiment of Zouaves and Garibaldi's forces, Agnus had emigrated to America in 1860 settling in New York. On the outbreak of war he had joined Duryée's Zouaves as a sergeant and was later promoted to second lieutenant. Agnus was wounded in the shoulder at Gaines' Mill, and while recovering was promoted to the rank of first lieutenant in the 5th. However, he had chosen to transfer to the 165th New York, where he had been commissioned captain of Company A, the colour company. Agnus had been

Shenandoah Valley campaign. Agnus claimed he received no fewer than 11 wounds in the war, and it was said that he had 'so much lead in him he rattled when he walked'.

5th New York Veteran Volunteers

The 5th New York Veteran Volunteers was the brainchild of Colonel Cleveland Winslow, who as acting major had commanded the original 5th New York at Second Manassas, where his horse had been shot from under him. Anxious that the good name of Duryée's Zouaves should not be lost, Winslow used his political influence and a 500-dollar grant from the New York stock

Recreated 5th New York Zouave on campaign in 1862. Fortunately he has managed to retain the complete Zouave dress. Hard campaigning and supply problems took a heavy toll on the 5th's uniforms, but the Zouaves patched and re-patched their famous baggy red trousers rather than give them up. Some 5th New Yorkers were in the habit of wearing the turbans they wore on parade in the field, but this Zouave is content to wear his fez unadorned. (Photo: Paul Smith)

slightly wounded in the 165th's attack on the earthworks at Port Hudson, and promoted to major he led a hand-picked forlorn hope in the final assault on the stronghold.

After the Confederate surrender at Port Hudson, the 165th served in western Louisiana and even skirmished with the legendary Confederate cavalry outfit Terry's Texas Rangers. During a hand-to-hand duel with a mounted Ranger, Agnus was badly slashed across the wrist. The 165th later served with Grant's forces in Virginia, and in 1864 they took part in Sheridan's

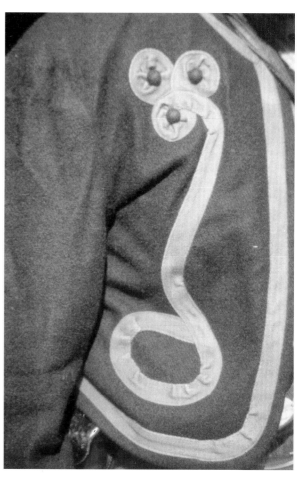

Close-up of a 5th New York jacket. The jacket is edged in red tape which has also been used to form the distinctive trefoil designs called tombeaux on each side of the chest. These tombeaux are a distinctive feature of Zouave dress. (Photo: Paul Smith, courtesy Tim Newark, Military Illustrated)

Lieutenant Thomas W. Cartwright, who commanded Company G, 5th New York, was nicknamed 'The Fiend' because of the way he treated the men. One of his favourite ways of punishing misdemeanours was to hang offenders up by their thumbs. Wounded at Gaines' Mill, Cartwright suspected he had been shot by a vengeful 5th New Yorker and not the enemy. (New York Division of Military and Naval Affairs)

exchange to raise a veteran regiment. Winslow's mother, Katherine Fish Winslow, was a cousin of the New York politician Hamilton Fish, and his father, Gordon, had been regimental chaplain of the original 5th New York.

Recruiting for the new regiment went slowly. Winslow unsuccessfully petitioned the Secretary of War to transfer the 5th New Yorkers whose time had not expired and were serving with the 146th New York into his veterans, but recruits from the original regiment and elsewhere did not come flooding in. A fanatical disciplinarian, Winslow had not been a popular officer, and many war-weary 5th New Yorkers were loath to serve under him again. As a whole, the North was becoming disillusioned with war, and in New York there were draft riots, which Winslow helped to suppress, swearing in 982 volunteers and 'borrowing' a battery of 12-pound howitzers to fight the mob.

Winslow offered bounties to attract recruits for the 5th Veterans, borrowing heavily to finance his dreams. 'My determination was fixed that the 5th Regiment should be preserved as the same organisation, cost what it would,' he wrote.

Eventually Winslow was able to put together a four-company battalion of 328 men, and for seven months his unit served in the defences of Washington. He set about instilling an *esprit de corps* with a vengeance. The men were rigorously drilled, especially in bayonet exercises and skirmishing by bugle call. All this, though, did not stop the 5th Veterans from enjoying the distractions of nearby Alexandria. Drunkenness became a problem in the battalion, and with typical zeal Winslow punished those who went astray by imprisoning them in Alexandria's old slave quarters. He ordered that Zouave inmates should be given three cold shower baths every 24 hours while they were incarcerated in the dungeon-like building.

In May 1864 the 5th Veterans were ordered south to join the Army of the Potomac engaged in the costly assault against Richmond. Winslow immediately asked that his regiment be put under the command of Major General Gouverneur Kemble Warren, a former 5th New York commander and the man who had saved the Union army's left flank at Gettysburg the year before by rushing troops to Little Round Top. Winslow also asked that his regiment be immediately posted to the front. Both requests were granted.

The 5th Veterans were placed in Ayres' 1st Brigade, 1st Division, Warren's V Corps. They reached the command camped on the Pamunkey River after two days' hard march. The battalion was immediately bolstered up to 10 companies with men from the mustered out 14th Brooklyn

Captain Churchill Cambreleng who commanded Company H, 5th New York, was commended for his gallantry during the Seven Days campaign in the Virginia Peninsula, but had to resign when his health failed. In this photo he wears an officer's version of the standard 5th New York Zouave jacket, which has been decorated with gold braid and which Cambreleng wears over a buttoned and braided vest. (New York State Archives)

and 12th New York whose terms of service had not expired. Winslow was itching for action. When General Ayres suggested resting the regiment after their long march, Winslow would have none of it. 'We came here to fight and not to rest,' he said, and the 5th Veterans were soon in the thick of the action at Bethesda Church, clambering through thick undergrowth clearing away enemy skirmishers.

Mounted, Winslow was a tempting target for the Confederates, and a bullet tore through his left shoulder, shattering bone. Managing to stay in the saddle, he was led to the rear as Ayres' brigade was flanked, falling back in disorder. The cost to the 5th Veterans was dear: 67 men and five officers killed or wounded and 35 captured.

Winslow had his wound dressed, and although in great pain he refused to leave the field until ordered to the field hospital by General Warren. Evacuated to the Mansion House hospital in Alexandria, Winslow lingered for a few weeks and then died.

Winslow's death was all the more tragic because his father, Gordon, drowned in a bizarre accident on the steamer *Mary Ripley*, while travelling with his wounded son to hospital. Leaving his son to rest, Gordon Winslow had gone out to get a pail of water for his horse, and slipped overboard at the mouth of the Potomac River. While Cleveland Winslow's death and his burial at Greenwood Cemetery in Brooklyn didn't generate the same hysteria as Ellsworth's demise, the gallant young officer was much lauded. The *New York Times* said Winslow had been 'strikingly handsome and attractive, marked by every noble and true trait which makes the gentleman-soldier'.

'Always Ready'

Elmer E. Ellsworth had wanted his Fire Zouaves to be the first Zouave regiment mustered in for the war, but instead the honour went to the 9th New York Volunteer Infantry, Hawkins' Zouaves, who were mustered into Federal service on 23 April 1861. The founder of Hawkins' Zouaves was Rush C. Hawkins, a military enthusiast and book collector whose collection of 15th-century books and manuscripts was said to be rivalled only by the British Museum.

Hawkins' Zouaves had their origins in a prewar military club formed in New York in 1860. Sergeant Louis Benzoni, a regular soldier, was appointed as Hawkins' Zouaves' drill master, and the regiment had a hard core of men with military experience. Hawkins himself had served as a dragoon in the Mexican war, and Major Edgar Kimball had been breveted for gallantry in the Mexican conflict while serving with the 9th US Infantry.

The motto of Hawkins' Zouaves was *Toujours Pret* ('Always Ready'), and the regiment would never be found lacking. They first saw combat in August 1861, at the capture of Fort Hatteras and Fort Clark on the North Carolina Coast, and made a spirited bayonet charge during an attack on Roanoke Island in 1862. Then came the bloody conflict at Antietam: after wading through

Antietam Creek the 9th mounted a steep ridge against ferocious resistance. 'The infantry fire was like hail around and among us, producing the most dreadful carnage,' wrote Lieutenant Kimball. The 9th's advance cost them dearly, with 240 men falling out of a total of 373 in the eight-company-strong regiment.

Swedish-born Private Charles Johnson, who wrote a regimental history of the 9th New York, *The Long Roll*, was hit twice in the hips in the course of the battle. 'What a picture that was to paint on my memory, our boys thinned down to a company, still carrying their colours triumphantly,' he recalled. Johnson was still suffering pain from his wounds when he died in 1896 at the age of 53.

10th New York

The 10th New York, National Zouaves, was another Zouave regiment that had existed as a pre-war organisation in the city. It was formed after calls from the *New York Herald* in 1860 for Northern patriots to band together against the threat of war, and many members were active in the Masonic fraternity. Waters W. McChesney, a former member of Ellsworth's United States Zouave Cadets, was appointed as drillmaster, and became the 10th's colonel. The 10th were mustered into service in late April 1861 for two years. For a time the unit was known as McChesney's Zouaves, but McChesney later resigned his position.

The regiment was renowned for the agility of its men. Many of its members were small, but wiry. 'No estimate has been made of the average age of the members of the tenth, but probably no regiment left New York State with a more boyish lot of soldiers,' wrote Charles W. Cowtan in his book *Services of the 10th New York Volunteers (National Zouaves) in the war of the rebellion*. 'As a rule they were small in stature, yet lithe and active, and handled guns and knapsacks with an elastic vigour which often put to blush regiments of six footers.'

Serving in Virginia, the 10th was brigaded with the 5th New York in Sykes' Division, Army of the Potomac. At Second Bull Run the regiment was positioned next to the 5th New York, and was also hit by the terrible attack from Longstreet's Corps.

The National Zouaves suffered 133 casualties and their regimental colours were captured by the 18th Georgia. Like the 5th New York, the wiry Zouaves of the National Zouaves saw some of the toughest fighting of the war.

Colonel Cleveland Winslow was the last commander of the 5th New York, and although comparatively soberly dressed here, he was renowned for his taste in extravagant uniforms, including a gaudily decorated Zouave jacket. 'Altogether he was half Italian bandit and half English highwayman, a romantic looking fellow,' remembered 5th New York veteran Thomas Southwick. Winslow created the 5th New York Veteran Volunteers, and was mortally wounded leading his men at Bethesda Church in 1864. (Brian Pohanka)

The Fighting 69th

Formed in the 1850s, the 69th Regiment New York State Militia was Irish-American to a man. Its colonel was Michael Corcoran, the son of a British army officer who had grown up in Ireland and served with the Irish Constabulary before emigrating to America. In 1860 Corcoran refused to parade the 69th in front of the Prince of Wales who was visiting New York, claiming the Prince was a symbol of British oppression. Corcoran risked a court martial for his stand; but with the outbreak of the Civil War in 1861, the action against him was dropped.

Irish nationalist Thomas Francis Meagher had been banished to Tasmania by the British government but he escaped to New York and became a US citizen. A lawyer and skilled orator, he campaigned widely for Irish independence. Like many Sons of Erin who had made America their new home, Meagher saw the coming civil war not only as a chance for thousands of Irishmen to prove themselves in their adopted country, but also as a valuable training ground for a much dreamed of showdown with Britain for the freedom of Ireland.

Not only was Meagher a patriot, he was also a glory seeker. There was a vacancy for a new company to be added to the ranks of the Fighting 69th, as the Irishmen became known, and Meagher set about recruiting a company of Zouaves, who became Company K of the regiment. The company was known as the Irish Zouaves or Meagher's Zouaves, and swaggered a little more than their comrades – who, for the most part, were attired in regulation Union dress.

At First Bull Run in 1861, where many of their compatriots in the Fire Zouaves were broken, Company K put up a much better fight, as the 69th faced stout resistance from Confederates who had captured Henry House Hill. Facing heavy fire, the 69th screamed murderous Gaelic war cries as they plunged up the slope; but each of their three courageous attacks was driven back. John Keefe of Meagher's Zouaves was carrying the 69th's distinctive green regimental colours in the fight, when a rebel tore them from his hands. Outraged, Keefe snatched them back and shot the Confederate dead. Keefe also managed to capture

Drum major John H. Naylor, of the 5th New York Veteran Volunteers, in 1864. The way turbans and fezzes were worn in the 5th New York Veteran Volunteers was an exacting science. Colonel Winslow ordered that the men's hair should be kept short so that their fezzes would sit neatly on the back of their heads and the turban should be worn 'canoe style' as shown here. The jackets of the 5th Veterans were of a lighter shade of blue than those of the 'Old Fifth'. (Michael J. McAfee)

a Confederate flag in the mêlée; some compensation for the 69th being ordered back from their attack on Henry House Hill.

Fresh Confederate troops had arrived, outflanking the Union right. In the retreat from Henry House Hill, Meagher was knocked head over heels and left unconscious on the field. He

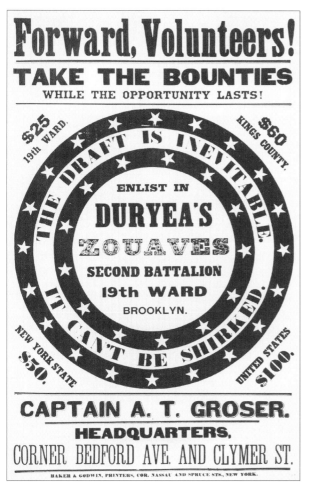

An eye-catching poster for the Second Battalion, Duryée Zouaves who were designated the 165th New York and shipped out to Louisiana. The combination of wearing Zouave dress and the bounties paid to join the regiment meant the 165th didn't go short of recruits. Lurid posters like this one were a popular method of attracting recruits during the American Civil War. (Michael J. McAfee)

an artillery wagon. But Meagher's troubles weren't over. One of the wagon's horses was shot and the wagon tumbled into Cub Run, pitching Meagher into the water. Despite his mishaps, Meagher staggered back to Washington with the battle-weary 69th, who won much praise for the fight they put up at First Bull Run. Even the Southern press acclaimed them. 'No southerner but feels that the sixty ninth maintained the old reputation of Irish valor,' gushed the *Memphis Argus*.

Corcoran spent 13 months in Southern prisons before being released in an exchange of officers around the middle of August 1862. He then raised a new Irish unit, Corcoran's Legion, but fresh

Private, 165th New York, Second Battalion Duryée Zouaves. The 165th was a very effective outfit, and this man looks every inch a Zouave. Just visible on the left edge of his jacket is the numeral '2' and the company letter 'F'. He's an exceptionally well turned out individual. (Michael J. McAfee)

was rescued by a trooper of the 2nd US Dragoons, who managed to haul the burly Irishman up across his saddle. Corcoran, the 69th's commander, had not fared well either: attempting to rally a last ditch defence against the advancing Confederates, Corcoran had formed the 69th into square. But panic was spreading throughout the entire Union army and in the shambles of the army's retreat Corcoran was captured.

Meagher, meanwhile, had recovered from being knocked out and fell in with a number of retreating Fire Zouaves, before he hitched a lift on

glories were to be short-lived for the dashing Irishman: he was killed after falling from a high-spirited horse at Christmas 1863; he may have been drunk at the time.

Using the 69th New York and recruiting other Irish-American regiments, Meagher went on to raise the Irish Brigade. Renowned for his love of battle, as well as drink, elaborate parties and horse racing, Meagher lived up to all the ideals of a true Zouave – on and off the field. He saw his beloved brigade grow into one of the greatest legends of the Civil War.

ZOUAVES EAST & WEST

Like the 69th New York, many early war militia units boasted companies of Zouaves. There didn't seem to be a city or town in the North where Zouaves couldn't be found.

'Oh we belong to the Zoo-Zoo-Zoos,
Don't you think we oughta?
We're going down to Washing-town
To fight for Abraham's daughter'

So ran a popular marching song of the war, belted out lustily by brave volunteers. But although Ellsworth and his Zouave Cadets had popularised Zouaves in America, some companies were already well established before the Zouave craze gripped the nation.

Cosmopolitan New York City, with its high proportion of French immigrants, boasted the Gardes Lafayette, who, complete with a company of Zouaves, became the 55th Regiment, New York State Militia, led by Philip Regis Denis De Trobriand, a French nobleman. Lionel Jobert D'Epineuil, who claimed to be a French army veteran, tried to raise another regiment of 'genuine' Zouaves from New York's French population, but most were already serving with other regiments, and the 53rd New York only mustered 130 true Frenchmen into its ranks.

Company B of the Brooklyn Greys, the 13th

Colour corporal Theodore d'Eschambault of the 165th New York, who was killed during the assault on Port Hudson, the Confederate stronghold on the Mississippi River. Note that Colour Corporal d'Eschambault has wrapped his sash in such a way that he has two end pieces hanging down over his leg; this must have been a real challenge to achieve with the unwieldy six-foot-long sash he was issued with. (Brian Pohanka)

New York State Militia, wore a natty Zouave uniform, while the Albany Zouave Cadets, who became Company A of the 10th Regiment, New York State Militia, wore a uniform heavily influenced by the United States Zouave Cadets. The Boston Light Infantry of Massachusetts, an old established independent company, had worn traditional uniforms including bearskin caps, but mothballed them in 1861 in favour of bright new Zouave uniforms. The illustrious Salem Light Infantry, founded in 1805, received Zouave

The most famous of the western Zouave regiments was the 11th Indiana Volunteer Infantry, Wallace's Zouaves, founded by Lew Wallace, a young lawyer, author and Mexican War veteran. Some of the 11th Indiana Zouaves also fought mounted in 1861, at a lively skirmish with Confederates near Romney, Virginia, a town they had previously liberated from the Confederates but which was now re-occupied by rebels.

A party of 13 mounted scouts from the 11th Indiana, commanded by brave Corporal Hay, were ordered to scout the area, and they ran into a

Lieutenant Charles R. Carville of Company D, 165th New York, was also killed during the assault on Port Hudson. He was only 19 at the time of his death and would have had a promising career ahead. In this photograph, Carville wears a frock coat and distinctive red Zouave officer's trousers. (Michael J. McAfee)

Swedish-born Gustav F. Linquist had originally signed on as a private with the 5th New York, but had a dramatic rise through the ranks, becoming a second lieutenant in the 165th New York in the winter of 1862. In this picture, Linquist wears a fez. Note the unusual pattern of the tombeau, just visible on the breast of his jacket. (Michael J. McAfee)

uniforms and renamed themselves the Salem Zouaves when they served as Company I of the 8th Regiment, Massachusetts Volunteer Militia.

Even the sober citizens of the North's western states were quick to respond to the Zouave allure. Several Zouave units flourished in Ohio and Indiana, including the 34th Ohio Volunteer Infantry, Piatt's Zouaves. Fighting on horseback, they galloped into action during a skirmish in West Virginia in 1861. They were wearing tricorne hats as part of their Zouave uniforms, and must have looked a truly bizarre sight.

A group of 10th New Yorkers pictured in this **Harper's Weekly** *illustration at their camp at Sandy Hook, New Jersey. Although they were impressively known as McChesney's Zouaves after their commander Colonel Waters W. McChesney, he proved unpopular and a deputation of officers successfully petitioned to have him removed from command. The 10th New York, popularly known as the National Zouaves, was said to have had some of the fittest men in New York serving in its ranks. (Ron Field)*

Confederate cavalry patrol of 41 troopers. The plucky corporal led his men in a desperate charge that killed eight rebels. Hay was wounded three times in the fight, but managed to stay on his horse and get back to safety.

The rest of his command were attacked by another force of Confederates, numbering around 60 men. The Zouaves made a stand on an island in the middle of a creek, and as night fell the rebels tried to sweep them off it. There was desperate hand-to-hand fighting, but the Zouaves held their ground, accounting for another 20

Confederates. After dark the Zouaves quietly waded through the creek and crept back to camp. Remarkably, they had lost only one man, killed in the hot fight on the island.

Wallace had set about raising the 11th Indiana as soon as he heard about the firing on Fort Sumter, the first act of the bloody drama of the Civil War. Recruiting posters were put up all over Indiana and brave volunteers flooded in. The 11th had nearly the same effect as Ellsworth's dashing United States Zouave Cadets. The 11th's snappy Zouave drill, devised by Wallace, attracted plenty of spectators. In her book *The Soldier of Indiana in the War for the Union*, historian Catherine Merrill wrote that Wallace's Zouaves were 'tall, erect, in the bloom and vigor of young manhood. Their appearance would have been striking without the aid of the showy uniforms'.

The original 11th was a three-month regiment, and when its term of service expired Wallace recruited another 11th Indiana that saw action in both the western and eastern theatres of the Civil War, fighting at Fort Donelson, Shiloh, Champion's Hill, Vicksburg and the Shenandoah Valley. Wallace became a major-general, the youngest Union officer to hold the rank, but he is better known for writing the novel *Ben Hur*.

NEW JERSEY ZOOS-ZOOS

New Jersey has a reputation for producing tough streetwise characters, and during the American Civil War many of them were attracted to the state's two Zouave regiments. Raised in late 1863, the two regiments were the 33rd and 35th New Jersey Volunteers; and if the attraction of wearing a fancy Zouave uniform wasn't a big enough pull, the large bounty offered to potential recruits was. However, several recruits went AWOL with the cash after they joined up. Captain Augustus Angel of the 35th New Jersey also had to deal with a drunken brawl among some of his men, and shot dead a private who came at him with a bayonet. The 33rd New Jersey, Mindil's Zouaves, commanded by Colonel George Washington Mindil, and the 35th New Jersey, Cladek's Zouaves, commanded by Colonel John J. Cladek, certainly had fighting spirit; it just needed to be directed at the enemy, not at each other.

Both regiments were sent west, and joined Sherman's army in the gruelling onslaught against Atlanta. The 33rd was the first of the two regiments to see action, flanking Confederates over steep inhospitable ground at Rocky Face Ridge in Georgia – an action where Colonel Mindil was wounded. At the Battle of Reseca, in May 1864, the 35th New Jersey with the 25th Wisconsin supported Morgan Smith's division of the XV Corps. The 33rd and 35th New Jersey saw a good deal of service through the Atlanta Campaign. The 35th became particularly adept at skirmishing; but Captain Angel, the officer who had been forced to shoot a Cladek's Zouave private in self defence, was killed by a rebel bullet. Both regiments suffered heavy losses: out of a total of 526 men,

The Burnside Zouaves, who hailed from Rhode Island, even wore white kepis as part of their spectacular looking uniform; but they were a short-lived outfit, only serving for five months in the summer of 1862 as a company with the 10th Rhode Island regiment. This dogged looking Burnside Zouave, Sergeant J.B. Gardner, poses kepi in hand. His jacket is light blue and the trousers red. (Michael J. McAfee)

the 33rd New Jersey could barely muster 200 at the end of the campaign.

Soldiering did have its compensations for the streetwise New Jerseymen of both regiments. The 33rd and 35th took part in Sherman's march to the sea, and were particularly good at foraging and 'liberating' valuables from the beleaguered Southern population. From an unpromising start, the roughneck Zouaves of the 33rd and 35th New Jersey had a very creditable war record, and proved themselves in more than one tough fight. Anyone who disagreed that they'd put on a good show would have been wise to keep his thoughts to himself.

THE AVENGERS

Following the untimely death of the gallant Ellsworth, at the hands of tavern-keeper James Jackson, the Ellsworth Association was formed, setting out to raise a regiment to honour the name of the gallant Fire Zouave commander.

'The grief of the people of New York at the villainous assassination of the noble Ellsworth is universal,' ran an editorial about raising the regiment in the *Albany Evening Journal.* 'Let the people of New York, his native state, mingle with their tears practical points for avenging his death.'

The Ellsworth Association's idea was that recruits should represent every town and ward in the state, with each town and ward donating money to provide arms and equipment for the volunteers. Recruits came from far and wide, and revelled in the regiment's name, Ellsworth's Avengers. The 44th was also known as the People's Ellsworth Regiment, but this title didn't have quite the same ring.

Recruits did not simply sign up for the 44th; they were nominated by patriotic citizens and had to fulfil certain requirements. Each Avenger had to be aged under 30 and stand not less than five feet eight inches tall. They had to be of sound moral character and preferably teetotal – ideals that reflected the conditions Ellsworth had laid out for the United States Zouave Cadets. Men of the 44th New York averaged 22 years of age, and

This determined-looking character is Private John Langdon Ward of the Salem Zouaves, who became Company I of the 8th Regiment Massachusetts Volunteer Militia. Pistols and knives stuck under belts was a macho display favoured by many volunteers early in the war when they had their photographs taken. John Langdon Ward was obviously out to impress. (Michael J. McAfee)

many were over five feet 10 inches tall. The Avengers certainly lived up to the expectations of the Ellsworth Association, and saw hard combat throughout the war. Serving in Butterfield's Brigade, Porter's Division Army of the Potomac, the 44th formed a quick attachment to the 83rd Pennsylvania, another 'showcase regiment', and the two outfits became known as 'Butterfield's Twins'.

Later transferred to Colonel Strong Vincent's Brigade, the 44th took part in all the major battles

Ethan A. P. Brewster had served in the Salem Zouaves before he became captain of Company A, the 23rd Massachusetts Volunteer Infantry, and it seems that Company A wanted to surpass the Salem Zouaves in splendour. Worn in this picture by an unidentified Zouave, Company A's uniform with its ornate tombeaux low on the jacket front and the tasselled sash, would make any Zouave proud. (Michael J. McAfee)

of the eastern theatre. At Malvern Hill the 44th made a spirited bayonet charge, spectacularly recalled by Avenger Lieutenant-colonel James C. Rice in his report on the battle. 'Onward the Forty Fourth marched in regular line of battle, with its colors far advanced, passing line after line of our troops who loudly cheered our flag as we steadily and firmly pressed on, till at length beyond the extreme front of our forces and within 100 yards of the enemy the regiment was ordered

to charge bayonets upon his line. Scarcely had the regiment charged 50 yards towards the enemy before his lines broke and fell back.'

It is claimed that the 44th lost 12 colour bearers between the time it started service and the Battle of Fredericksburg, in December 1862. One ragged flag, retired after Fredericksburg because it had seen so much service, was riddled with 84 bullet holes and badly torn by shells. The flag pole had twice been cut in two by musket-balls.

Ellsworth's Avengers saw their hardest fighting at Gettysburg, when they were one of the regiments of the 3rd Brigade, 5th Corps, rushed to Little Round Top to stop the Union left flank being rolled up by the Confederates. Colonel Rice of the 44th requested that his regiment be placed next to its 'twin', the 83rd Pennsylvania. This was granted, and the 44th was placed on the right of the 83rd Pennsylvania and the left of the 16th Michigan, who had been moved from their original position next to the 83rd. On the far left was the 20th Maine.

An early casualty of the 44th was Captain Lucius S. Larabee, the commander of Company B and a former United States Zouaves Cadet, who was shot after advancing his company as skirmishers. Scrambling up Little Round Top came seething lines of rebels, but with its oblique fire to the right, the 44th helped check the advance, and held their ground firmly until the charge of the 20th Maine down Little Round Top crushed the Confederate attack. During the fight for Little Round Top, Strong Vincent, the 3rd Brigade's commander who had given permission for the 44th and 83rd to stand together, was killed and Colonel Rice of the 44th took over command.

Little Round Top was a dearly bought victory for the 44th and its brother regiments, the 20th Maine and the 83rd Pennsylvania. (The 16th Michigan had disgraced itself by breaking too easily.) The greatest cost to the 44th was in Company A, who lost 21 of the 40 men they had taken into battle. Apart from Captain Larabee, many officers of the 44th were mortally wounded, including First lieutenant Eugene L. Dunham of Company D and Second lieutenant Benjamin N. Thomas of Company K. But the enemy had also paid a heavy price. After witnessing the carnage of

This picturesque scene is an encampment of the 11th Indiana, Wallace's Zouaves, the most famous Zouave unit to come from the western states. Here the men wear the regiment's first uniform, which was grey with red facings. A man with strong Christian beliefs, Colonel Lew Wallace is said to have chosen this rather constrained uniform so as not to emulate the North African Moslem origins of Zouave dress too much. (Michael J. McAfee)

The second uniform of Wallace's Zouaves isn't so well known as the first, but lasted the regiment until the end of the war. It featured a dark blue jacket and intriguing tombeaux design. Here it is worn by Private John L. Cook of Company G. (Michael J. McAfee)

the aftermath of Little Round Top, battle-weary Sergeant E.R. Goodrich of Company A, Ellsworth's Avengers wrote: 'At night of July 2 our company was on picket in our front at the foot of the hill. The ground was literally covered with dead and wounded. It was the worst picket duty I ever performed. I spent all my time, while on picket, attending to the wounded…It was terrible, some crying some praying some swearing and all wanting help.'

During that hot day at Gettysburg and throughout the war, Ellsworth's Avengers certainly lived to up to their title.

PROUD PENNSYLVANIANS

In August 1861 Irish-born lawyer Captain Charles H.T. Collis raised a company of Zouaves in Philadelphia as a bodyguard for General Nathaniel Banks. Dubbed the Zouaves d'Afrique, Collis and his men proved their mettle during a rearguard action fighting off Confederates during the retreat of Banks' army at Middletown, Virginia. Collis and his Zouaves were cut off from the main Union army, but made it back to the lines, bringing with them 40 wagonloads of much-needed supplies which they had escorted to safety.

The Zouaves d'Afrique, who had the initials 'ZDA' proudly displayed on their cartridge box plates, were a particularly fine looking outfit. The company also boasted a gourmet chef, Private Nunzio Finelli, whose exquisite soufflés were very popular with Captain Collis.

In recognition of his valuable services, Collis was despatched back to Philadelphia to raise a full regiment of Zouaves, and in just over a month nine companies of the 114th Pennsylvania were formed. One of those who enlisted was Robert Kenderine. He faced fierce opposition from his Quaker family, but thought it was his duty to help preserve the Union and abolish slavery. From the 114th Pennsylvania's training ground at Camp Banks, near Germantown, Robert wrote to his parents: 'My country is now calling loudly for succor. I yield. I assure you I have acted from stern duty.'

At Fredericksburg in the winter of 1862 the 114th Pennsylvania charged straight into a Confederate counter-attack, which helped save the Federal left flank from disaster. Encouraging his men, Collis snatched up the colours on horseback and rode with them among his cheering Zouaves. Collis, who was then only 24, later received the Medal of Honour for his gallant action.

At Gettysburg Collis' Zouaves took 50 per cent casualties, mostly on the second day, when they were part of the Third Corps over-extended battle line. Advancing across the Emmitsburg Road near the Peach Orchard, to help cover the retreat of a Federal battery from an onslaught by Barksdale's

The 34th Ohio, Piatt's Zouaves, build a bridge across a creek in western Virginia. Some of the men can be seen wearing tricorne shaped hats, a curious form of Zouave dress to be sure. Piatt's Zouaves were very innovative. Not only did they build bridges, but some served mounted in a skirmish with the enemy. (Michael J. McAfee)

Colonel John J. Cladek was in command of the rough streetwise Zouaves of the 35th New Jersey, Cladek's Zouaves, an outfit which sometimes seem to have frightened its own side as much as it did the enemy, but emerged to be a first class fighting unit. The 35th New Jersey were issued Hawkins' Zouave uniforms, which had become the government standard issue. (Michael J. McAfee)

Mississippi Brigade, the 114th ran into heavy opposition. They were reinforced by men of the 73rd New York, fellow Zoos-Zoos who were grandly known as the 2nd Fire Zouaves. Together, the 114th and 73rd faced withering fire from the frontal and flank attacks made by the Rebels. Some wounded Zouaves crawled into a nearby barn for safety, but they were burned to death when the building went up in flames.

The day afterwards, a Confederate officer surveyed the carnage in the Peach Orchard and wrote: 'Many dead Federal soldiers were lying, conspicuous among them Zouaves with baggy red trousers.'

Among the 114th's wounded at Gettysburg was Private Kenderdine, the man who had defied his parents to become a Zouave. His wound was mortal and a week after the battle he died. The 114th went on to serve at Kelly's Ford, Mine Run, Guinea Station and the trenches at Petersburg. In 1864, in honour of their 'discipline and soldierly bearing', General Meade selected the 114th Pennsylvania as his headquarters guard and the 114th's musicians became the headquarters band. Colonel Collis was breveted brigadier-general and commanded the headquarters brigade. The 114th became showpiece soldiers, but nobody looked down on them. They had earned respect throughout the Army as tough troops.

Apart from Collis' famed Zouaves, Pennsylvania produced four more memorable Zouave outfits: the 23rd Pennsylvania (Birney's Zouaves); the 72nd Pennsylvania (Baxter's Fire Zouaves); the 76th Pennsylvania (Keystone Zouaves); and the 95th Pennsylvania (Gosline's Zouaves). The 72nd was recruited in Philadelphia, and like the 11th New York was composed of firemen. It seemed that firefighters in the North were particularly fascinated with the idea of becoming Zouaves, and within a week the muster rolls of the 72nd Pennsylvania were full.

Baxter's Zouaves, commanded by Colonel De Witt Clinton Baxter, became part of the Philadelphia Brigade, an outfit mainly recruited in central Pennsylvania and also comprising the 69th, 71st and 106th Pennsylvania Volunteers. On the second day at Gettysburg the 72nd helped recapture an artillery piece of the 1st Rhode Island Artillery that had fallen into enemy hands and the morning of 3 July found the Philadelphia Brigade stationed by the stone wall at the Angle, where they faced the onslaught of Pickett's Charge.

The 72nd had been held in reserve to cover the space occupied by Cushing's battery, in case the battery was knocked out, but they were ordered into action to reinforce the 71st and 69th Pennsylvania. A single Confederate volley cut down at least 80 Zouaves, but musket fire from the 72nd is said to have accounted for the death

help stop the Confederates at the stone wall, said they deserved to have their monument placed in the exact spot where they'd helped fight back the Confederate high tide. After a lengthy fight in the courts, they won their case and in 1891 the statue was proudly placed in the Angle. Baxter's Fire Zouaves' had won their last fight.

The celebrated Keystone Zouaves of the 76th Pennsylvania Volunteer Infantry saw action miles from home, on the Carolina coast. They were garrisoned at Hilton Head in South Carolina, and were involved in assaults on Fort Wagner, a Confederate stronghold guarding Charleston Harbour and a place more readily associated with the gallant assault made by the coloured volunteers of the legendary 54th Massachusetts Regiment, commanded by Colonel Robert Gould Shaw.

In July 1863 the Keystone Zouaves and other units of General George C. Strong's brigade

The 44th New York, Ellsworth's Avengers, were the pride of New York state and lived up to their spectacular name. This private wears his jacket buttoned and just visible on the top of his cap are the initials 'PER', standing for People's Ellsworth Regiment, the other name by which the 44th was known.(Michael J. McAfee)

of the Confederate general Richard Garnett near the wall.

The statue of a 72nd Pennsylvania Zouave using his musket as a club is one of the most spectacular at Gettysburg, but getting it located in the Angle was a problem for the veterans of Baxter's Fire Zouaves. To stop the Angle getting crowded with monuments, the Gettysburg Battlefield Memorial Association ruled that regiments who fought in the area could only erect monuments where each regiment had first been located. However, the 72nd Pennsylvania, who had been held in reserve before rushing up to

Dying in Washington on 23 March 1862, Private James Davis had a short career as an Avenger. His jacket is unbuttoned in this studio photograph, revealing what could be one of the specially made shirts issued to the unit. (Martin L. Schoenfeld)

advanced through hellish Confederate fire and struggled on to Fort Wagner's parapet. For a few glorious moments it seemed as if victory could be in the grasp of the gaudily clad Zouaves, but amid desperate tenacious fighting the Union troops could not maintain their foothold and were sent reeling back. The Keystone Zouaves lost 180 men. During another assault on the fort, a week later, they were hurled back again, and Fort Wagner remained impregnable to Union troops until September 1863.

Transferred back to the eastern theatre, the 76th saw action in the Virginia campaign of 1864, including Cold Harbour, the Crater and Petersburg – but some rueful veterans of the regiment thought that none of these actions compared with the hell the Keystone Zouaves went through at Fort Wagner on the humid Carolina coast.

THE BLOODY WILDERNESS

During 1863 and 1864 three Union regiments who had previously been clad in regulation army dress were issued Zouave uniforms as a reward for their proficiency at drill and to maintain the proud Zouave legacy. The delighted recipients of these fancy new uniforms were the 146th New York who received their Zouave dress in June 1863, followed by the 140th New York and the 155th Pennsylvania, who were issued with Zouave uniforms early in 1864.

These three Zouave regiments formed half of a brigade commanded by Brigadier-general Romeyn B. Ayres. In the 146th's ranks were many three-year enlistees from the legendary 5th New York, transferred from Duryée's Zouaves because their terms of service had not expired.

The new Zouave uniform was particularly welcome to the men of the 155th Pennsylvania. When they were mustered into service in 1862, they had been issued ill-fitting long blue coats and armed with unreliable Belgian rifles. The new Zouave uniforms, issued in January 1864, helped

Period sketch of the Zouaves d'Afrique, also known as Banks' Bodyguard, a company of Pennsylvania Zouaves raised by Captain Charles H.T. Collis. He was later authorised to recruit a full regiment of Zouaves in Philadelphia, which became the 114th Regiment Pennsylvania Volunteer Infantry, the famed Collis' Zouaves. (Library of Congress)

to instill fresh pride in the men of the regiment.

Also issued with its Zouave uniforms in early 1864 was the 140th New York, one of the regiments who had fought in the fierce contest for Little Round Top at Gettysburg, during which their commander, Patrick Henry O'Rorke, had been killed.

In the Wilderness campaign of 1864, when Grant's army became entangled with the Army of Northern Virginia in acres of Virginia scrub and forest, the three regiments of Ayres Brigade would see some of the toughest fighting of the war. One of the few open spaces in the dense undergrowth of the wilderness was an area known as Saunders Field, around 800 yards long and 400 yards wide. It was there that Union troops pitched into General Richard Ewell's Confederates. Leading the Union advance was the 140th New York with the 146th in the second line. The 140th was com-

started with an ear-splitting yell that echoed through the woods, giving assurance to the troops on the right and left of the line that Ryan's Zouaves were charging the enemy,' wrote Captain Henry Cribben of the 140th. The lines of colourful Zouaves didn't falter, even though a stray shell from a Union battery ploughed into the back of the 140th.

Collis' Zouave in a picture taken around 1863. He's posing without gaiters or jambieres, and the comparative narrowness of his Chasseur, rather than Zouave pattern, trousers can be seen. For such a relaxed shot it's strange that this private wanted to wear his turban, usually reserved for full dress occasions.(Michael J. McAfee)

manded by O'Rorke's successor, Colonel George Ryan. They'd managed to keep good order while struggling through the undergrowth, and welcomed being in the open until they were hit by fierce Confederate fire.

Waiting for reinforcements, Ryan, whose horse had been hit, ordered his men to lie down. Fresh troops arrived to bolster the line, and Ryan ordered his Zouaves to charge. 'The regiment

No-nonsense looking Captain Francis Fix, of the 114th Pennsylvania, proudly wears his regiment's numbers in the officer's insignia on his kepi. Fix saw tough action with the 114th at Gettysburg, where he was wounded. Fix was invalided out of service during Christmas 1863. (Michael J. McAfee)

THE SECOND FIRE ZOUAVES OF NEW YORK.

The 73rd New York Volunteer Infantry proudly called themselves the 2nd Fire Zouaves, and for a time at Gettysburg fought alongside the 114th Pennsylvania. Seeing service throughout the war, the 73rd had a much more illustrious career than Ellsworth's First Fire Zouaves, who virtually ceased to exist after First Bull Run. As shown in this Harper's Weekly *print, the Second Fire Zouaves wore Chasseur-type dress with dark blue jackets. Dark blue forage caps were worn, although at least one period photograph shows the 73rd wearing fezzes. (Ron Field)*

Waving his hat, Ryan led the cheering Zouaves into the woods which bordered the other side of Saunders Field. Amongst the undergrowth the lines of determined Zouaves dissolved into groups and began to push their way forward, clawing at the enemy. 'Closing with the enemy we fought them with bayonet as well as bullet,' recalled Captain H.W.S. Sweet of the 146th. 'Up through the trees rolled dense clouds of battle smoke, circling about the green of the pines. Underneath men ran to and fro, firing shouting, stabbing with bayonets.'

But it was impossible to pull off an effective attack in such difficult terrain, and Ryan was forced to pull his men out of the woods and retreat back over the killing ground of Saunders Field, which they'd marched so resolutely across. 'The bright red of our Zouave uniforms mingled with the sober gray and butternut of the Confederates, creating a fantastic spectacle as the wearers ran over the field, firing and shouting,' wrote one Zouave.

On that hot afternoon in the Wilderness, on 5 May 1864, the fight at Saunders Field had cost the 140th and 146th New York 567 men out of their combined strength of 1,600. During the Sanders Field fight, the 155th Pennsylvania had been battling it out with rebels in woods to the north, in what proved a less costly but equally hard contest. All the men of the three new Zouave

United States Zouave Cadets, 1860
1: Colonel Elmer E. Ellsworth
2 & 3: Cadets

WRv 95

A

11th New York Volunteer Infantry, 1st Fire Zouaves, 1861
1 & 2: Privates

B

11th New York Volunteer Infantry,
1st Fire Zouaves (Second Uniform), 1861
1: Officer
2 & 3: Privates

C

Tiger Rifles, Company B, 1st Special Battalion Louisiana Infantry, Bull Run, 1861
1: Corporal
2 & 3: Privates

D

1: Private, Charleston
Zouave Cadets, 1861
2: Private, Albany
Zouave Cadets, 1861
3: Corporal, Salem
Zouaves, 1861

E

1: Private, Irish Zouaves, Company K, 69th New York State Militia, 1861
2: Corporal, New York Volunteer Infantry, Hawkins' Zouaves, 1862
3: Sergeant, 10th New York Volunteer Infantry, National Zouaves, 1862

F

Gaines' Mill, 1862
1: Private, 5th New York Volunteer Infantry, Duryée's Zouaves
2 & 3: Sergeant John H. Berrian and Sergeant Andrew B. Allison, 5th New York

1: Officer, 11th Indiana Volunteer
Infantry, Wallace's Zouaves, 1861
2: Private, 11th Indiana Volunteer
Infantry, Wallace's Zouaves, 1863
3: Private, 76th Pennsylvania Volunteer
Infantry, Keystone Zouaves, 1863

H

Pennsylvania Zouaves, 1863
1 & 2: Private and Vivandière,
72nd Pennsylvania, Baxter's Fire Zouaves
3: Sergeant, 23rd Pennsylvania, Birney's Zouaves

WY 95

I

165th New York, 2nd Battalion,
Duryée's Zouaves, 1864
1 & 2: Officers
3: Private

1: Private, 44th New York, Ellsworth's Avengers, 1864
2: Private, 140th New York Volunteer Infantry, 1864
3: Sergeant, 146th New York Volunteer Infantry, Garrard's Tigers, 1864

WB/95

K

1 & 2: Private and Vivandière,
114th Pennsylvania, Collis' Zouaves, 1864
3: Private, 155th Pennsylvania
Volunteer Infantry, 1864

WR/95

L

regiments in Ayers' Brigade had worn their new Zouave uniforms with honour.

SOUTHERN TIGERS

Standing six feet four and weighing a hefty 275 pounds, Roberdeau Wheat was an imposing figure. He needed all his strength to control the 1st Special Battalion Louisiana Infantry, better known as Wheat's Tigers. The son of an Episcopalian minister, Virginian-born Wheat was a lawyer and soldier of fortune. He had served as an officer in the Mexican war and fought in Cuba and Central America as a member of Walker's freebooting expeditions.

After serving with Garibaldi's forces in Italy, Wheat had returned to America on the eve of the Civil War. General Winfield Scott, his former commander, had asked him to serve the Union, but Wheat's sympathies lay with the South, and he went off to seek a commission in the Confederacy. None was available, so Wheat went back to his old stamping ground, New Orleans, and raised a company of volunteers called the Old Dominion Guards, who became part of the 1st Special Battalion, Louisiana Infantry.

Wheat was later elected major of the 1st Special Battalion, an outfit that also boasted a company called the Tiger Rifles. Pretty soon the entire 1st Special Battalion, Louisiana Infantry became known as Wheat's Tigers.

The Tigers became one of the most infamous outfits ever produced by the South, and boasted a number of colourfully named companies. Planters' sons of the Catahoula Guerrillas rubbed shoulders

One of the best photographs of Civil War Zouaves ever taken is this group of Collis' Zouaves. These turbaned Zoos-Zoos are Company G of the 114th Pennsylvania photographed at Petersburg in 1864. All the men have the look of proud veterans, and it's little wonder that General Meade selected the regiment to be his headquarters guard. (Michael J. McAfee)

Many photos of the 23rd Pennsylvania, Birney's Zouaves, show enlisted men wearing kepis with red trim, but this Zouave sports a fez and tassel. The metal object on the front of his fez is unclear. Perhaps it's his regiment's numerals or some kind of badge. (Michael J. McAfee)

with the soldiers of fortune of the Walker Guards, and dispensing justice with his fists was the sergeant of the Tiger Rifles, a former prizefighter who found that sorting out troubles in the battalion gave him plenty of opportunities to brush up his skills.

Rascals they may have been, but Wheat's Tigers never lacked courage in their brief but memorable Civil War service. At First Bull Run Wheat's Tigers were situated on the Confederate left flank at the Stone Bridge, with the 4th South Carolina Volunteers of Colonel Nathan Evans' brigade. Advancing a mile upstream from the bridge, to hold back the enemy who were bearing down on the Confederate left and buy time for reinforcements to arrive, the Tigers took the full force of a flanking movement launched by Ambrose Burnside's Rhode Island Brigade, who outnumbered the feisty Zouaves six to one.

The South Carolinians came up from the Stone Bridge in support of the Tigers, but in the smoke and confusion of battle mistook them for Yankees and fired a volley into their ranks. Outraged, the Tigers fired a volley back before order was restored. The Confederates were slowly being pushed back, but there was still plenty of fight left in the Tigers. Dismounting from his horse, Wheat drew his sword and waved it in the air to rally his scattered men. But at that moment Wheat was hit by a musket-ball. It struck him underneath his upraised arm, pierced his lung and passed completely through his body.

A group of Tigers rolled their stricken leader on to a blanket and started to carry him to the rear. Wheat survived the perilous journey to the field hospital, even though he was dropped on the ground when two of the men carrying him were shot. The Tigers left in action faltered when they heard about their leader, but they soon rallied, and their stout defence was stiffened by the arrival of two Confederate brigades. Shouting Wheat's name, the Tigers charged the Yankees. It was claimed that several Tigers even dropped their muskets and went at the Union troops just flourishing their wicked Bowie knives.

With First Bull Run ending in a Confederate victory, Wheat's Tigers, who had held Burnside's Yankees at bay until reinforcements could arrive, became the heroes of the hour. Meanwhile Wheat was languishing from his wound. A surgeon said he wouldn't survive the night, but in reply Wheat said that he would make a full recovery from his wound; to his men's delight and the astonishment of his doctors, he did.

One of General Ewell's aides had not been impressed by the Tigers at Bull Run, and rather foolishly he voiced his opinions. Defending the Zouaves' honour, Captain Alex White, the commander of the Tiger Rifles company, challenged him to a duel. The men didn't choose pistols or swords, but rifles – blazing away at each other until General Ewell's aide fell mortally wounded, hit just above the hips. Celebrating White's victory, the Tigers ran amok in Lynchburg, Virginia. They also engaged in frequent brawls with soldiers from Kentucky and Georgia.

While Wheat was out of action recovering from his wound, Lieutenant-colonel Charles de Choiseul was put in temporary command of the Zouaves. Determined to tame the Tigers, he had two unruly Zouaves sentenced to death. 'Whether the Tigers will devour me, or whether I will succeed in taming them remains to be seen,' he wrote. The two men facing execution were reputedly part of a gang that had beaten up an officer and tried to rescue some imprisoned Tigers.

Wheat was outraged and argued for clemency, especially since one of the condemned men had been a member of the party that had carried him to safety at Bull Run. But his pleas fell on deaf ears; on 9 December 1861 the two Zouaves were shot by a firing squad made up of their fellow Tigers. Excused from watching his men die, Wheat sobbed quietly, alone in his tent.

By the time of Jackson's Valley campaign, in the spring of 1862, Wheat was fully recovered, but he was still embittered by the execution of the two Tigers. He and his Zouaves had lost none of their reckless spirit, however. At Front Royal the Tigers rushed across a burning railway bridge to get at the enemy, before helping to chase the Yankees through the town. Later the Tigers were part of a force also comprising some of Turner Ashby's cavalry and the Rockbridge artillery pursuing retreating Federals toward Winchester. Gleefully the Tigers kept up with the fast pace of the trotting horses.

In June 1862, Wheat's Tigers took part in what was to become their last great fight, at Gaines' Mill, the same battlefield where the red-legged Yankees of the 5th New York were engaged. As if foreseeing that this fight would cost him his life, Wheat became melancholic on the eve of the

Colonel De Witt Clinton Baxter gave his name to Baxter's Fire Zouaves, the 72nd Pennsylvania. Baxter looks like the archetypal military figure here and wrote a book called **Zouaves Light Infantry Tactics**; *but like so many Civil War officers, Baxter was a civilian turned soldier. Before the war he worked as a wood engraver and customs official. Here he appears to be holding a McDowell-style forage cap, and it looks like he's wearing a regulation officer's overcoat with cape. (Michael J. McAfee)*

battle, and ordered he be buried where he fell.

During the battle Wheat's Tigers were one of the units struggling across Boatswain's Swamp, taking part in an attack on the Federal right. Wheat rode ahead of his men to encourage them, but close to the Federal lines he was shot through the eye and died instantly. The death of Wheat meant the Tigers couldn't be rallied, and they broke. 'They have killed the old major and I am going home,' cried one tearful Tiger. Without Wheat, the Tigers were no longer an effective fighting unit, and the remaining battle-weary Zouaves were assigned to other regiments.

COPPENS' WILD ZOUAVES

The men of the 1st Battalion Louisiana Zouaves were as infamous as their counterparts in Wheat's Tigers. The unit was founded by George Auguste Gaston de Coppens, a leading New Orleans socialite who was authorised to raise his battalion by Confederate adjutant General Samuel Cooper. Coppens came from a noble French family, so it was natural that he should want his regiment to be Zouaves. His plans happily coincided with a theatre troupe proudly calling themselves the *Inkerman Zouaves*, who appeared on stage in New Orleans, setting the Gallic blood of many men in the city racing.

Coppens had the kind of reckless character appreciated by Zouaves. Before the war he had built up a formidable reputation as a duellist, fighting one affair of honour with opera critic Emile Bozonier. The latter had accused Coppens of making rude noises during a performance by two of his favourite opera singers, and called Coppens out. They engaged in a swordfight outside New Orleans. Coppens received a slash across his cheek, but won the duel, seriously wounding Bozonier.

The command structure of Coppens' Zouaves was very much a family affair. One of his brothers became a company commander, while another brother signed up as a sergeant. Coppens senior, Baron Auguste de Coppens, became the battalion's quartermaster. Some of the other officers of Coppens' battalion had wide military experience. Major Waldemar Hylested, a former Swiss citizen,

The Keystone Zouaves of the 76th Pennsylvania saw war on two fronts in both the western and eastern theatres. They had a particularly attractive uniform with a light grey 'false vest' shown particularly well by the sergeant with his jacket open shown here. On his sleeve he has a veteran's stripe, in recognition that he signed up again after his term of service expired. (Michael J. McAfee)

Sergeant Michael Lawn of the 95th Pennsylvania wears the regiment's simple but distinctive red-trimmed jacket and on the top of his kepi is a VI Corps badge. Jackets of similar design were worn by the 72nd and 23rd Pennsylvania. The ball buttons down the front of the 95th's jackets closely resembled the buttons designed by Ellsworth for the United States Zouave Cadets. (Michael J. McAfee)

could boast 16 years' military service. He had served in the French Army during the Algerian campaigns, and after emigrating to America served with the South Carolina Palmetto Regiment in the Mexican war.

Like Major Hylested, Captain Fulgence de Bordenave had seen service in Algeria, while Captain Paul F. DeGournay had been active in the Louisiana State Militia. After a flash flood of recruits into the ranks of Coppens' battalion, the supply of volunteers began to dry up, and it looked as though it was going to be difficult to fill the remaining two companies. Advertisements were placed in newspapers, and several of Coppens' men tried a more drastic method of recruiting by kidnapping and trying to impress innocent passers-by into the battalion. By hook or by crook the ranks were filled, and the battalion was sent to Pensacola, on the Florida coast. As the last company of Coppens' battalion was about to leave New Orleans, an elaborate ceremony was held outside City Hall. After a band had played the *Marseillaise* and distinguished citizen Charles M. Morse had presented a flag, Coppens' officers drew their swords which were then kissed by a group of New Orleans ladies. A knight going to the Crusades couldn't have hoped for a better send-off.

Coppens' battalion was one of the most cosmopolitan units in the Confederacy. About 20 per cent of the men were Swiss, but the regiment also had numerous Frenchmen, native born Americans, Germans, Italians, Spaniards, Irishmen and Englishmen in its ranks. William Howard Russell, a correspondent for the London *Times*, saw the Zouaves while they were stationed at Pensacola and was impressed. 'The men looked exceedingly like the real article,' he wrote. But the Zouaves would have to wait a while before they tasted glory. Much of their time at Pensacola was spent drilling and digging ditches.

In June 1861 Coppens' battalion left Pensacola for the long journey to Virginia. The chance of active service at last should have been appealing to the men, but there was trouble in the ranks. At Pensacola the battalion had been camped in a miserable mosquito-infested area, and they hadn't been paid since they'd enlisted. On the special

ment tried to restore law and order until Coppens' officers arrived. Setting about the men with a vengeance, the officers pistol-whipped and cajoled them back onto the train. But they did not settle down, and they ran wild in Columbia, South Carolina. Several Zouaves also died after pulling crazy stunts on the train, and one was shot dead by an officer trying to restore order.

As they passed through Petersburg, Virginia, one onlooker wrote to a friend that Coppens' Zouaves were 'the most savage-looking crowd I ever saw,' and when the Zouaves ended their long train journey, at Richmond, they were locked in on the second floor of a warehouse. Several of them managed to escape by tying their sashes

Albert Ross was transferred from the 5th New York to the 146th New York as one of the men whose term of service hadn't expired. Ross is pictured wearing a 5th New York jacket and 146th New York trousers, which could have been a tribute to his former regiment or reflect supply problems. (Brian Pohanka)

train taking them to Virginia the disgruntled men became riotously drunk. At Garland, Alabama, the train stopped and the officers got off to enjoy breakfast, leaving the men on the train. In scenes akin to a Keystone Kops silent movie rather than a genuine piece of Civil War history, the angry Zouaves uncoupled the officers' carriage and hijacked the train, chugging off to Montgomery.

The angry officers flagged down a locomotive and followed the Zouaves, who spilled out of their train at Montgomery, Alabama and ran amok. Local citizens and some men of a Georgia regi-

This Garrard's Tiger wears the full uniform of the 146th New York, with its particularly elaborate yellow tombeaux. All the newly created Zouave regiments in Ayres' Brigade relished their Zouave uniforms. 'We had the vanity to think there was no organisation in the army superior to us,' wrote one officer. (Martin L. Schoenfeld)

together, climbing out through a window and descending the wall.

A deputation of officers threatened to resign their commissions unless Coppens was removed from the leadership of the battalion and conditions improved. However, tempers were eventually quietened and the regiment was first in action as part of a force attacking Hampton, Virginia, in August 1861. Enjoying themselves immensely, the Zouaves set fire to many buildings in the town, but another period of garrison duty followed. The Zouaves would have to wait until 1862 for more action, when their thirst for combat would be quenched in a series of desperate fights with the enemy.

A Confederate soldier remembered Coppens' battalion as 'the most rakish and devilish looking beings I ever saw' – a statement that is certainly be believed in an account of a grisly incident that happened after the Battle of Williamsburg. One badly wounded Union prisoner was in terrible pain and asked to be put out of his agony; he was obliged by a Coppens' Zouave with his musket butt. He also asked if any other Yankee prisoners wanted to be accommodated in the same way.

But Coppens' men would earn respect for their tenacious fighting on the battlefield. At Seven Pines Lieutenant Colonel Coppens was wounded and half of his Zouaves were cut down. Then at Gaines' Mill Coppens' Zouaves were decimated again when they charged through Boatswain's Swamp, and Second Bull Run also cost them dearly. Like the rest of the 2nd Louisiana Brigade they were serving with, Coppens' men ran out of ammunition at Second Bull Run and they ended up hurling rocks at the enemy to try and keep them at bay.

Antietam was the last stand of the exhausted Zouaves. Lieutenant Colonel Coppens was killed in the terrifying fight along the Hagerstown Pike, and his men were reduced to a shadow of their former strength. After Antietam the battalion was reorganised, but it never saw serious combat again. Even so, the exploits of Coppens' Zouaves and their infamous reputation for playing as hard as they fought has never been forgotten.

ZOUAVE DRESS

The classic French Zouave uniform was based on the baggy trousers, short jackets and fezzes worn by the native North Africans when the French began recruiting Zouaves in the 1830s. The famous baggy Zouave trousers were called serouels and in their basic form they were no more than two large squares of cloth sewn together with openings for the legs.

The jackets were originally just trimmed with red on the edges, but by 1833 tape forming an elaborate clover leaf design and 'false pocket' called a tombeau was added to each side of the chest and the French also incorporated a vest into the uniform, which buttoned up at the top and sides and was worn under the jacket over a shirt. Many American Zouave units, though, were not content to follow this classic Zouave uniform style, and a bewildering variety of uniforms were adopted.

Even Elmer Ellsworth, the man at the forefront of the Zouave craze, did not outfit his men in traditional Zouave dress, a fact noted in a contemporary account describing the United States Zouave Cadets in the French newspaper *Courier des Etats Unis*. 'These Zouaves are, however, three-quarters contraband. Their uniform has little of the uniform of the French Corps whose name they have adopted. We looked in vain for the leggings of the Zouave, his puffy trousers that rest upon the calf of his leg.'

Following Ellsworth's example, a number of volunteer regiments adopted fanciful Zouave uniforms, while other units like the 5th New York Volunteer Infantry, Duryée's Zouaves, adhered closely to a true Zouave style. The real inspiration for the 5th uniforms most likely came from Felix Agnus. He had served with the 3rd Regiment of French Zouaves, and it is reputed that he wore his uniform when he enlisted with the 5th New York.

Zouave uniform designs were often decided by a regiment's board of officers on 27 April 1861. Most of these uniforms were made by Devlin Hudson and Company while the remainder were

Recreation of a Tiger Rifle Zouave on campaign in 1861. His drawn Bowie knife is shaped like a sword at the hilt. It could also be used as a first class 'knuckle duster' in close combat. Note the distinctive striped trousers, ubiquitous red shirt and the unusual striped socks. Wheat's men were the only Zouave unit North or South to wear such strange socks. (Photo: Michael Thomas)

manufactured by the William Seligman Company.

Complaints were made that the quality of the 5th first uniforms was not high and the cut of the trousers was too tight across the calf. The last 125 pairs of trousers delivered to the regiment were lengthened by two inches. The first uniforms of Duryée's Zouaves featured jackets with elaborate tombeaux designs joined up with the tape trim on the edge. Jackets adopted by the regiment around

February 1862 featured a tombeau design not linked up to the jacket edge.

The red felt fezzes worn by many Zouave regiments followed by a similar design to those worn by the 5th. The first red felt fezzes worn by the Duryée's Zouaves were made by the Seamless Clothing Company and had blue tassels, but in early 1862 yellow tassels were adopted. Zouave officers of most regiments wore red kepis gaudily decorated with gold braid, usually with a small brass regimental number fixed to the front. Officers wore frock coats, but unlike their French counterparts, their trousers were of a far narrower cut than the men's and more of a chasseur style. Zouave officers indulged in considerable freedom of dress, Abram Duryée, commander of the 5th New York, frequently sported a curious pill box shaped fez.

ZOUAVES IN SKIRTS

During the Second Empire no regiments of the French Army were complete without their 'daughters' – ladies armed with barrels of brandy who brought succour to the men and nursed the wounded. These women were known as cantinières or vivandières and several Zouave regiments in the American Civil War copied the idea.

The word vivandière is a combination of Latin and French, and literally means 'hospitality giver'. In France vivandières first made their appearance with the French Army in the 17th century, and the distinctive painted barrels carried by vivandières were adopted around the time of the French Revolution. Vivandières of the mid-19th century should not be confused with camp followers. They were an official part of the French Army and were sometimes married to soldiers in the ranks.

Vivandières, particularly those who served with the dashing Zouave regiments, excited considerable interest because of their colourful uniforms, and numerous illustrations were made of them wearing their modified feminine versions of

Thomas Francis Meagher sits with his beloved Irish Zouaves, Company K of the 69th New York State Militia. Taken in Washington in 1861, this rare picture of Company K shows Meagher's men to be a tough, soldiery bunch of characters, who were proud to be the only company in the Fighting 69th to wear Zouave dress. Meagher himself was fond of wearing a gold trimmed Zouave uniform, but surprisingly not for this photograph. (Michael J. McAfee)

Zouave dress. In the Crimean, Italian and Mexican campaigns of the French Army, several vivandières had notable service records. Madame Jouay of the 3rd Zouaves was present in all three campaigns, and Antoinette Trimoreau of the 2nd Zouaves received the Military Medal for saving the regimental eagle at Magenta. Jeanne-Marie Barbe of the Guard Zouaves also received the Military Medal during this battle.

Coppens' notorious Zouave battalion had two vivandières who caught the eyes of hot-blooded males when the regiment marched. A Tennessee captain bumped into one of the vivandières and wrote to his wife: 'Billy fell desperately in love with her and insists I shall turn my company into

LOUISIANA ZOUAVE PRISONERS IN THE GUARD-HOUSE AT FORTRESS MONROE.—[SKETCHED BY OUR SPECIAL ARTIST.]

This rare illustration of Confederate Zouaves, first published in **Harper's Weekly**, *on 27 July 1861, shows prisoners from Coppens' Battalion held at Fortress Monroe. Two of the Zouaves in this picture, Franz Minute and John Atzrodt, claimed to have deserted from the battalion en-route to their first posting at Pensacola. The reclining Zouave on the floor is lying on a rigid early war style militia knapsack and the men were said to be wearing 'a coarse Zouave uniform'. (Ron Field)*

a Zouave company and have two of them along.'

After First Bull Run, Lavinia Williams, a vivandière with Wheat's Tigers, appeared on stage in South Carolina to raise money for a sick Zouave in her care. Tickets cost 25 cents each, and apparently Lavinia put on a very good show, including demonstrating the knife fighting techniques of the Tigers. 'She is a very strong looking woman and tells with perfect nonchalance of killing Yankees and the like. You may depend on it, the children crowded to see her, dressed as she was in the gay costume of her vocation,' wrote the theatre critic of the *Edgefield Advertiser* in October 1861.

Vivandières also served with many Northern regiments: as early as 1853 the famed Old Greybacks of the 7th Regiment, New York State Militia had outfitted nine-year-old orphan Molly Divver as a vivandière and adopted her into the regiment. Vivandières joined a number of other regiments during the War, but the most famous Zouave regiment, the 5th New York, strangely never signed up any 'daughters'. Colonel Duryée received several applications from interested ladies, but all were rejected. One Emma L. Thompson wrote that she and a friend were 'exceedingly desirous of going out with some regiment'. She said that she could provide good references about the moral character of herself and her friend, but Duryée still wouldn't budge.

The most famous vivandière of the American Civil War was Marie Tepe (or Tebe). A French immigrant, Marie married Philadelphia tailor Bernado Tepe and followed him to war as a vivandière when he joined the 27th Pennsylvania Volunteers. Later Marie was asked to join the 114th Pennsylvania Collis' Zouaves by Collis himself, and she received a bullet in her ankle at Fredericksburg. After the battle she was awarded the famous Kearny Cross, a medal commemorating the fallen General Philip Kearny and given to brave members of the Union Third Corps. It is said that 'French Mary', as she became known, was present at 13 battles, and an officer of the 8th Ohio recalled seeing her at Spotsylvania in 1864. 'She was about 25 years of age, square featured and sun burnt. She was wonderfully courageous. Every sort of projectile falling in the midst of us was trying the nerves of our coolest.' French Mary survived the war and lived for a long time afterwards, but she committed suicide sometime around 1900. It seems likely her painful ankle-wound contributed to her sad demise.

EPILOGUE

At First and Second Bull Run, the tangle of the Wilderness and in many other battles, American Zouaves experienced glory and tragedy in equal measure.

The spectre of a Duryée's Zouave is sometimes said to appear at dusk near the regiment's monument at Second Bull Run where the 5th New York was overwhelmed by Hood's Texans; and whether you believe in ghosts or not, it is difficult not be affected by a sense of brooding that pervades the area.

Some historians have dismissed American Zouaves as nine-day wonders who disappeared in the early stages of the war, but Zouaves were to be found on battlefields throughout the conflict. The last Union soldier killed before Lee surrendered, at Appomattox Court House in 1865, was a young Zouave of the 155th Pennsylvania.

The Zouave ideal did not stop with the end of the war, many post-war militia units adopted Zouave dress. In 1868 men of the 6th Maryland Regiment proudly wore their new Zouave uniforms, complete with turbans around their fezzes, in a parade through Baltimore, marking the inauguration of a new steamship service between Baltimore and Bremen in Germany. In New York the National Guard boasted no fewer than three post-war Zouave regiments, some members wearing surplus Civil War Zouave uniforms.

Many original Civil War Zouave regiments

French Mary followed her husband to war and eventually became the 114th Pennsylvania's Vivandière, dispensing liquor and tobacco to tired soldiers. Few women in the 19th century experienced combat first hand like French Mary. Visible on her jacket is the Kearny Cross, one of the most highly prized awards of the Civil War. (Michael J. McAfee)

formed veterans' associations after the war, and the grand old boys of these organisations proudly wore their uniforms and carried their bullet-torn colours at parades well into the 20th century.

Glasgow-born Andrew Coats, a private with the 5th New York, emigrated to America in 1855 and was very active in veterans' affairs after the war until his death at 81 in 1921. Private Robert

Lieutenant Colonel Hiram Duryea was cheered by the 5th New York Zouaves at Gaines' Mill because of his coolness under fire. He lived for a long time after the war, only to be murdered by his lunatic son, Chester, who shot him seven times at the family's Brooklyn home in 1914 – an inglorious end to the tough old warrior's career. (New York Division of Military and Naval Affairs)

Sadler, of the 5th New York, was born in England in 1840. He was wounded at Manassas, but survived, dying in Los Angeles in 1923.

During and after the Civil War, Zouaves were soldiers with attitude, who added broad brush-strokes of colour to the rich canvas of American military history.

THE PLATES

American Zouaves may have been colourfully dressed, but for the most part their arms and equipment were standard regulation issue. With a few exceptions, Zouaves were armed with rifle muskets and wore the same basic equipment as their comrades in 'ordinary' volunteer regiments.

A: Colonel Elmer E. Ellsworth and his United States Zouave Cadets, 1860

Uniforms of American Zouaves varied, from almost exact copies of French Zouave dress to wide interpretations of the Zouave style. Even with his great interest in Zouaves, Ellsworth strangely did not choose to outfit his men in baggy pants and fezzes. Instead the United States Zouave Cadets wore uniforms that were colourful but which better resemble the Chasseurs of the French Army.

Being primarily a showcase unit, the Cadets had no fewer than four uniforms, which they frequently mixed and matched. Ellsworth (A1) is wearing his own version of the Cadets' Chasseur uniform, combining a double-breasted frock coat with red trousers. His red kepi trimmed with gold piping is typical of the fancy headgear sported by Zouave officers, but Ellsworth's kepi also has a regulation staff officer's hat badge with gold-embroidered oak leaves around a US logo embroidered in gold.

The Cadet (A2) standing by his illustrious leader is also bedecked in the formal-looking Chasseur uniform, a combination of the Cadets' dark blue frock coat and the trousers worn by A3.

His kepi is also the same style as that worn by A3, and the castle motif on A2's collar is a regulation engineer's collar insignia. It seems Ellsworth had his Cadets wear them on their Chasseur dress, either because he simply liked the design or because he planned to have an engineer company within the ranks of his Cadets, whose duties would include setting up tents. The castle insignia, which does not show up well in photographs, has been interpreted by some historians as a letter 'H' worn by the Zouave Cadets because

they were originally Company H of the 60th Regiment Illinois State Militia. But sketches Ellsworth made before the war clearly show that the collar insignia is a castle.

Figure A3 wears the 'Zouave dress' of the regiment, worn when the Cadets gave their snappy drill displays. The jacket is of a Zouave cut, and though baggy, the red trousers are Chasseur pattern; not baggy enough to satisfy Zouave purists.

Figures A2 and A3 carry militia knapsacks strapped to their backs. Made out of wood or pasteboard covered in black leather, these knapsacks are typical pre-war and early war issue. The stiff construction didn't provide any 'give', and they could be uncomfortable to wear. Figures A2 and A3 are armed with 1855 pattern rifle muskets with bayonets fixed for full effect. Another version of the Zouave Cadets' uniform featured the full dress frock coat, blue-grey trousers and white cross belts.

B: Privates, 11th New York Volunteer Infantry, 1st Fire Zouaves, 1861

These two toughs from the Fire Zouaves who

Uniformed 5th New York veterans in the early 1900s. Many American Civil War veterans' associations were active well into the 20th century, and some old newsreels show Zouaves on parade. The 'last man' of the 5th New York was British-born Private William H. McGuffage, who passed away in Chicago, Illinois, on 12 May 1940, aged 99. His war had long been over, but another one had just begun. (Brian Pohanka)

'invaded' Washington in the early summer of 1861 wear the regiment's first uniform. Funds to clothe the 11th New York had been raised by public subscription, and the uniforms were partly based on designs Ellsworth had made before the war. Again, they're of a Chasseur, rather than a true Zouave style.

The light grey jackets faced darkish blue with red edgings and the light grey trousers of coarse jean cloth material were very stylish; the uniform of Francis E. Brownell, the Fire Zouave who shot Ellsworth's killer down, can be seen at the Manassas battlefield visitor centre.

Figure B1's forage cap bears the brass numerals 'IZ' standing for 1st Zouaves, and above is the numeral 'A' denoting his company. On his jacket, which has 10 brass ball buttons down the front, like all his comrades in the Fire Zouaves, he has proudly pinned an 1860 pattern fireman's badge. His fire-fighting heritage is also reflected in the distinctive red fireman's shirt which can be seen underneath his jacket and in his belt, where the white letters spell out 'PREMIER', the name of his fire engine company back in New York.

Figure B1 carries a model 1855 rifle musket fitted with a sabre bayonet which he carries in his belt. Companies A and K of the Zouaves were issued with 1855 rifle muskets before the regiment left New York, while the rest of the Zouaves received various Sharps rifles. Dissatisfied with these rifles, considering them unsuitable for Zouaves, many members of the 11th New York refused to use them and received Springfield muskets as replacements.

Figure B2 relaxes nearby and, tossing his forage cap aside, reveals his shaved head. Before leaving New York for Washington, each Fire Zouave had a radical haircut; some went even further by having patriotic motifs, like Figure B2's American eagle, carved into the stubble. This style may have been influenced by the French Zouaves, who were renowned for shaving their heads.

The firemen's badges illustrated on this plate are typical of those worn by engine companies, hose companies and hook and ladder companies of the New York Fire Department just before the war – and displayed proudly by the men of the 11th New York.

C: 11th New York Volunteer Infantry, 1st Fire Zouaves (second uniform), 1861

This Fire Zouaves officer (C1) and two privates (C2 and C3) are pictured in the debacle of First Bull Run, where many men of the 11th New York, and indeed the rest of the Union army, broke and ran. These three men are made of sterner stuff, though, as they turn to face Jeb Stuart's cavalry.

The company officer (C1), who grimly holds the Fire Zouaves' colours, wears a single-breasted frock coat adorned with a row of seven New York buttons and gold braid loops on the cuff slashes. Shoulder straps are dark blue edged red. Some officers wore enlisted men's trousers in action, but Figure C1 wears full dress grey trousers with gold stripes edged in red. He has a model 1851 sword.

The grey uniform first issued to the Fire Zouaves (see Plate B) was of poor quality and quickly wore out. New uniforms were provided by the government, but to the 11th's disgust these were not of a Zouave pattern and the men refused to wear them. The government hastily issued red fezzes with blue tassels and a consignment of blue sashes was also delivered. Figures C2 and C3 wear these items and the dark blue trousers, which the Zouaves decided to keep from the first issue of replacement uniforms. C2 also wears a distinctive fireman's shirt.

A dark blue Zouave jacket was also issued, but details of this are unclear, and it seems it wasn't widely worn at Bull Run, where most Zouaves (like C2 and C3) fought in their shirt sleeves. C2 has retained the tan gaiters of the Fire Zouaves' first uniform and tucked his trousers into them, while C3 has dispensed with the gaiters and tucked his trousers into his socks. Both are armed with model 1855 muskets.

The magnificent colours carried by the officer were presented to the Fire Zouaves by the New York Fire Department. Measuring 68 by 54 inches, the colours were made out from white silk, with the details, including items of firemen's equipment, painted on. The staff has a metal halberd at the top which looks like a fireman's axe.

Saved from capture at Bull Run, the colours were placed in the collection of the New York State Division of Military and Naval Affairs after the war, but around 1960 they went missing. As this book was being written, the long-lost 11th New York colours, some of the most colourful carried in the Civil War, were found rolled up in a cardboard box. As this book went to press, the colours hadn't been unrolled because the silk could be very fragile, and their future had yet to be decided.

D: Tiger Rifles, Company B, 1st Special Battalion Louisiana Infantry, Bull Run, 1861

Taking part in the action against Burnside's Rhode Island Brigade at Bull Run, these three Zouaves epitomise the fearsome reputation of the Tiger Rifles, who were probably the only company in the 1st Special Battalion dressed as

Zouaves. Figure D1 is a Tiger corporal who wears the unit's blue Zouave jacket decorated by tombeaux in red tape. It has been claimed that the Tiger Rifles were issued both blue and brown jackets, but in fact blue was the only issue. Some jackets quickly weathered and faded to a brown colour because of the poor quality of the dye.

Figures D2 and D3 have discarded their jackets, and many Tigers, like the trio depicted here, wore red shirts, possibly inspired by several Tigers (including their commander, Roberdeau Wheat) who had served with Garibaldi's famed 'Red Shirts' before the Civil War. The blue striped trousers are the most distinctive part of the Tiger Rifles' uniform, and it is said they were made out of hard-wearing bed ticking.

Figure D1 and one of the Tiger Rifles privates (D2) have tucked their trousers into gaiters, while the other private (D3) has tucked his trousers into distinctive striped socks that wouldn't look out of place on a modern day basketball player.

One contemporary account says that the red fezzes with blue tassels worn by the Tiger Rifles resembled skull caps, and some devil may care Tigers, like D3, adopted the habit of wearing straw hats, sometimes with a patriotic motto on the headband. The Tigers were armed with 1841 pattern Mississippi rifle muskets, a very distinctive looking weapon. But D2 has dropped his musket, preferring to go at the Yankees with just his Bowie knife. This rugged veteran with the eyepatch has a Colt revolver tucked underneath his waist-belt.

E1: Private, Charleston Zouave Cadets, 1861
The Charleston Zouave Cadets were a company of 'Southern Zoos-Zoos' who became a part of the First Regiment of Rifles South Carolina 1st Regiment of Rifles. These smart young volunteers from some of the best families in Charleston were inspired by the ideals Ellsworth had drummed into the United States Zouave Cadets. If they were seen even entering a bar, they were thrown out of the company, but the compensation for staying sober was this smart grey uniform trimmed in red and cut in a Chasseur style. Note the kepi with a small crown. Some Cadets favoured wearing a small brass palmetto tree

insignia on their kepis. The Cadet is armed with an 1841 pattern Mississippi rifle musket.

E2: Private, Albany Zouave Cadets, 1861
The smart Albany Zouave Cadets also heavily imitated the United States Zouave Cadets, and they later became Company A, 10th Regiment, New York State Militia. His kepi carries the brass numerals 'AZC' and note how the figure's trousers are baggy at the top and taper downwards. His black leather waist-belt carries the ever popular 'SNY' belt buckle which Confederates are alleged to have claimed stood for 'Snotty Nosed Yank' and not 'State of New York'.

E3: Corporal, Salem Zouaves, 1861
Arthur F. Deveraux was a former business partner of Elmer E. Ellsworth, and when the former was elected captain of the Salem Light Infantry, in 1861, the unit was quickly transformed into the Salem Zouaves. The smart new Zouave uniforms, with trousers, vests and jackets made out of navy blue woollen twill fabric, were delivered in June 1861. Interesting features of this uniform include the collar trimmed in red leather and the unusual-looking gaiters which have lace-up outer seams secured by a white porcelain button. Figure E3's kepi bears the initials 'SZ', but some Zouaves still carried the old Salem Light Infantry initials, 'SLI', on their headwear.

F1: Private, Irish Zouaves, Company K, 69th New York State Militia, 1861
The only distinctively Irish feature of Meagher's famed Zouave company was their green sashes. Their jackets were standard Zouave style with red tombeaux. It was thought that Company K wore green vests underneath their jackets, but as illustrated on Figure F1, they were blue with red trim like the jackets. Caps and trousers were of the same style as those worn by the rest of the 69th New York.

The rest of Figure F1's uniform is standard and this Zouave fights barefoot, a Gaelic habit which some members of the 69th indulged in at First Bull Run.

Against the heat he's covered his forage cap with a white cloth havelock. Originated by British general Sir Henry Havelock and worn by British soldiers in the Indian Mutiny, havelocks were popular with troops in the early stages of the Civil War. Figure F1's is a part of a consignment sent by patriotic New York ladies.

Company K were reported to have been armed with pattern 1816 muskets rifled and converted to the Maynard primer system. Figure F1, though, has chosen to arm himself with an 1842 pattern smoothbore musket, the main arm of the 69th.

F2: Corporal, 9th New York Volunteer Infantry, Hawkins' Zouaves, 1862

Hawkins' Zouaves never wore baggy red trousers, but a matching uniform of blue trousers and jacket. These trousers were always of a narrower cut than the truly voluminous Zouave style, and when the regiment was formed the men wore straight trousers and jackets without tombeaux. By 1862, though, the United States Quartermaster Department was issuing Hawkins' Zouaves uniforms like the one worn by Figure F2. His jacket is trimmed with red tape and a narrow strip of red cord at the edge. This uniform became standard issue for other regiments, including the 164th New York. Surplus 9th New York uniforms were also worn by some post-war Militia units.

F3: Sergeant, 10th New York Volunteer Infantry, National Zouaves, 1862

From 1861 to 1862, the National Zouaves were issued with no fewer than three different uniforms. The first, made out of dark blue flannel, quickly wore out and the second, though in heavier material and featuring a brown jacket, fared little better. The distinctive third uniform, shown here, was a great improvement. Note the unusual red and gold down the trousers and the regimental cap plate attached to the front of his turban. Some National Zouaves sported these plates on their turbans, a feature unique to the 10th New York.

G1: Private, 5th New York Volunteer Infantry, Duryée's Zouaves, 1862

Of all Civil War Zouave regiments, Duryée's Zouaves were one of the most authentically dressed. When foreign war observer General Prim of the Spanish Army inspected the 5th New York, he said they looked exactly like the 2nd Regiment of French Zouaves. G1 wears his dark blue jacket over a distinctive shirt vest a strip of red tape running down the middle. His baggy trousers are cut in the full Zouave style, based on the baggy trousers known as *serouels* worn by native North Africans. In their most basic form, *serouels* were simply two large pieces of cloth joined together, with openings for the legs. His trousers are tucked into jambieres, gaiters laced up with leather thongs and worn over white gaiters. His waist sash has been wrapped in such a way that the inverted 'V's at the end of the sash hangs down over his left leg.

Wrapping their sashes this way was a 5th New York speciality. His fez is trimmed with a thin strip of yellow tape on the bottom – also a feature on many fezzes worn by other Civil War Zouave regiments.

G2 & G3: Sergeant John H. Berrian & Sergeant Andrew B. Allison, 5th New York, Gaines' Mill, 1862

Maddened by the death of his brother, killed earlier at Gaines' Mill, Sergeant Berrian (G2) has snatched up the 5th New York's regimental colours and marched 50 paces in front of the 5th's line to defy the enemy. Inspired by this action, national colour bearer Sergeant Andrew B. Allison (G3) has come up to stand by his side.

Union regiments carried both regimental and national colours, and the 5th New York's regimental colour carries the coat of arms of New York with the regimental inscription '5th N.Y.S.V.' in gold on a red scroll. The 5th New York NCOs wore Zouave uniforms with distinctive gold trimming. Figures G2 and G3 have gold sergeant's stripes on a red background. They have gold chevrons on their cuffs and their tombeaux are also edged in gold.

H1: Officer, 11th Indiana Volunteer Infantry, Wallace's Zouaves, 1861

The more sober nature of western Zouave regiments is depicted in this grey uniform, based on an original illustration of Colonel Lew Wallace. 'There was nothing of the Algerian colours in the uniform, our outfit was of the tamest grey,' wrote Wallace about the first clothes of his regiment. But with his flowing havelock, Zouave jacket and white trousers tucked into black boots, Wallace still manages to look pretty spectacular.

H2: Private, 11th Indiana Volunteer Infantry, Wallace's Zouaves, 1863

Strangely, the first grey uniform of Wallace's Zouaves is better known than the second uniform Figure H2 is outfitted in, which the regiment wore for a longer time. The later uniform was adopted around December 1861, and the men served in it for the rest of the war. They wore their original red forage caps until they were replaced with blue ones, and the very dark blue Zouave jackets featured distinctive 'drooping flower' tombeaux on the chest, variations of which are common in the uniforms of several western Zouave regiments. Trousers were standard army issue blue kerseys, often worn tucked into tan coloured gaiters.

H3: Private, 76th Pennsylvania Volunteer Infantry, Keystone Zouaves, 1863

The 76th Pennsylvania and the Collis' Zouaves were the only Pennsylvania Zouave regiments who wore close approximations of Zouave dress. The light blue trousers and dark blue jackets made the 76th's uniform particularly attractive. It was furnished by the Schuykill arsenal in Pennsylvania. An unusual feature of the jacket is the false sky blue vest front stitched into it.

I: Pennsylvania Zouaves, 1863

This plate is an informal grouping of two of Pennsylvania's other Zouave regiments. Figures I1 and I2 are a private and vivandière from the 72nd Pennsylvania Baxter's Fire Zouaves, while Figure I3 is a sergeant from the 23rd Pennsylvania, Birney's Zouaves.

Baxter's Zouaves wore dark blue jackets trimmed with red over elaborately trimmed shirts or vests. Figure I1 wears a sky blue vest under his jacket which is ornamented with brass ball buttons. Baxter's Zouaves wore either the regulation forage caps or McClellan Chasseur style kepis. Their trousers were light blue and had

smart red stripes running down the side seams.

The vivandière sports a jaunty blue 'liberty cap' styled on woollen caps worn by patriots in the American Revolution. She wears a Zouave jacket and a skirt slipped over a pair of regulation infantryman's sky blue trousers. The vivandière's jacket displays a green hospital steward's chevron, but in case of trouble she also carries a small sword and pistol at her belt. Moving on to the sergeant, the elaborate tombeaux at the bottom of Figure I3's jacket was a distinctive feature of Birncy's Zouaves, as was the delicate piping on the cuffs. The sergeant has a sash around his waist as a mark of rank.

J: Officers and Private, 165th New York, 2nd Battalion Duryée Zouaves, 1864

The extravagant privately purchased uniforms worn by Figures J1 and J2 make standard Zouave uniforms look positively tame. The illustration of Figure J1 is based on the jacket worn by Felix Agnus, second commander of the 165th New York. This spectacular uniform was tailored by Brooks Brothers in New York, who imprinted their label on the trouser buttons. The jacket is positively laden with red tape and gilt trim, with sleeves slashed to the elbow and secured by 10 brass buttons.

The kepi, with a scarlet top and black band, has a gilt-embroidered posthorn on the front enclosing a silver 'Z'. The rust red trousers are heavily pleated at the top and have gilt decorations around the pocket. The trousers are worn over a pair of gaiters, a habit popular with Zouave officers.

Figure J2 wears a more subtle uniform, but for all that it's still spectacular. Note that the top of Figure J2's kepi is higher than Figure J1's, and the visor displays a gilt chin-strap. The jacket again features elaborate red and gilt trim, and of special interest is the elaborate detail around the shoulders. Figure J2's white vest has brass buttons set off with a bow tie, and his trousers are also worn over white gaiters.

Figure J3 is on guard duty. 165th New York Zouaves were only allowed to wear turbans on guard or at the special request of officers. They were also expected to keep their equipment scrupulously clean, and could be fined 25 cents for not having shiny brasswork. His shirt vest, with a single button at the neck, bears the brass initials 'D' and 'Z' of his beloved regiment.

K1: Private, 44th New York, Ellsworth's Avengers, 1864
The uniform of the famed Avengers was certainly heavily influenced by those worn by the Albany Zouave Cadets (see Plate E). The 44th was a distinctive-looking regiment: note the red shirt with its light blue trim. He has been fortunate in retaining the full Zouave uniform including the dark blue Chasseur pattern trousers with red stripes; some Avengers had to wear the regulation New York fatigue uniform also issued to them because hard campaigning meant their Zouave uniforms wore out. Photos taken in Alexandria, Virginia, in 1864 show some Avengers wearing their Zouave jackets with regulation light blue trousers. No Zouave ever gave up his uniform easily.

K2: Private, 140th New York Volunteer Infantry, 1864
This proud private, a veteran of the fight at Saunders Field, chooses to wear his fez with the bottom trimmed in yellow tape turned up. The 140th were one of the Union regiments 'transformed' into Zouaves late in the war, and wore their uniforms with pride until the end. 'The cloth is by far better material than any clothes issued before,' wrote one private. 'It is of good quality – the color dark blue trimmed with red.' Another private said he thought the uniform was 'the easiest and most comfortable dress worn'.

K3: Sergeant, 146th New York Volunteer Infantry, Garrard's Tigers, 1864
The new uniforms received by the men of the 146th New York were the style worn by the Tirailleurs Algeriens, or Turcos, of the French army – native colonial troops who fought with the same tenacity as Zouaves. The light blue uniform trimmed in yellow shown here is very similar to a classic Zouave uniform, but the trousers lack quite the same bagginess. Colonel Kenner Garrard of the 146th was ordered to Washington to oversee

the production of the uniforms and the men were extremely happy with them. The regimental historian wrote that the 10-foot long waist sash provided the men with 'great comfort and warmth'.

L1: Private, 114th Pennsylvania, Collis' Zouaves, 1864
The 114th Pennsylvania were a particularly fine looking outfit, and as Meade's Headquarters Guard at the end of the war they were also one of the most photographed Zouave regiments. This Zouave is dressed in classic 114th style. His jacket is trimmed with red worsted lace tombeaux, daintier than the red tape used by other Zouave uniforms. Also note the delicate red cord trefoils above the blue cuffs. Until original 114th uniforms were unearthed, the colour of the cuffs couldn't be verified, because the light blue registered white in period photographs.

Collis' Zouaves' trousers were of a narrower Chasseur pattern than traditional Zouave trousers, colourfully ornamented with yellow designs around the pockets.

L2: Vivandière, 114th Pennsylvania, Collis' Zouaves, 1864
This figure is based on the dress of French Mary, the Civil War's most famous vivandière. She wears a standard 114th Pennsylvania jacket and a civilian hat decorated with feathers. Her skirt is worn over 114th red Chasseur trousers, and she carries the classic trademark of vivandières, a small barrel used to dispense nips of liquor to tired soldiers. On her belt she carries a holstered pistol, but whether French Mary ever had to use hers is not known.

L3: Private, 155th Pennsylvania Volunteer Infantry, 1864
Part of the 155th's uniforms were manufactured and imported from France, but they weren't originally intended to be Zouave uniforms. The American government had imported 10,000 French Chasseur à Pied uniforms, but the jackets were found to be too small for brawny Americans. Some of the larger-sized Chasseur trousers were suitable for a Zouave regiment, though, and they

went to the 155th Pennsylvania. Completing the outfit, the capes supplied with the Chasseurs à Pied uniforms were converted into Zouave jackets for the 155th Pennsylvania. Bright yellow tombeaux were added to these jackets, and false vest fronts were stitched in. The result was an unusually attractive uniform, popular with the men. 'The exchange to the Zouave uniform from the plain blue infantry uniform was enjoyed immensely,' wrote the regimental historian. Figure L3 wears a blanket roll over his shoulder, a method popular with Civil War soldiers for carrying their blankets, with personal effects rolled up inside.

BIBLIOGRAPHY

Davenport, A., *Camp and Field Life of the Fifth New York Volunteer Infantry, Duryée Zouaves,* Dick and Fitzgerald, New York 1879. Reprinted by the Butternut Press, Gaithersburg, Maryland, 1984.

Nash, E.A., *A History of the Forty Fourth Regiment New York Volunteer Infantry,* Chicago 1911. Reprinted by the Morningside Bookshop Press, Dayton, Ohio, 1988.

Cowtan, C.W., *Services of the 10th New Volunteers (National Zouaves) in the War of the Rebellion,* New York, 1882.

Johnson, C., *The Long Roll, Impressions of a Civil War Soldier,* New York, 1911.

Under the Maltese Cross, Antietam to Appomattox, 155th Regimental Association, Pittsburgh, 1910.

Conyngham, D.P., *The Irish Brigade and its Campaigns,* Boston, 1869. Republished by Ron R. Van Sickle Military Books, Gaithersburg, Maryland, 1987.

History of the Second Battalion Duryée Zouaves, 165th New York Volunteer Infantry Regimental Association, New York, 1904.

McAfee, M.J., *Zouaves, The First and the Bravest,* Thomas Publications, Gettysburg, 1991.

Echoes of Glory, Arms and Equipment of the Union, Time-Life Books, Alexandria, Virginia, 1991.

The Company of Military Historians, Long Endure: The Civil War Period 1852-1867, Presidio Press, Novato, California, 1982.

Jones, T.L., *Lee's Tigers,* Louisiana State University Press, 1987.

Notes sur les planches en couleurs

A Le Colonel Elmer E. Ellsworth et ses United Zouave Cadets 1860. Bizarrement, Ellsworth ne choisit pas d'habiller ses hommes en pantalon bouffant et fez comme les vrais Zouaves mais ses hommes portaient un uniforme qui ressemblait plus à celui des Chasseurs de l'armée française. Ellsworth, A1, porte sa propre version de l'uniforme des Cadets Chasseurs avec un pardessus à double boutonnage et un pantalon rouge. A2 porte également l'uniforme des Chasseurs des United States Zouave Cadets alors que A3 porte l'Uniforme Zouave' du régiment porté lorsque les Cadets faisaient des parades d'exercice.

B Ces deux Zouaves de la 11ème New York Volunteer Infantry, les 1st Fire Zouaves, portent le premier uniforme du régiment avec une légère veste grise aux parements bleu foncé et un pantalon gris clair. Le calot de la figure B1 porte les numéros en cuivre '1FZ' qui signifient 1st Fire Zouaves et la lettre de cuivre 'A' qui indique sa compagnie. La figure B2, assis sur le trottoir, s'est rasé la tête et un aigle a été sculpté dans ses cheveux en brosse. Ces coupes de cheveux hors du commun étaient peut être influencées par les Zouaves français qui avaient la réputation de se raser la tête.

C Un officier des Fire Zouaves et deux troupiers représentés à la bataille de First Bull Run. L'officier C1, qui tient avec détermination l'étendard des Fire Zouaves, porte un pardessus à boutonnage simple alors que les deux Zouaves portent le second uniforme des Fire Zouaves. Ces uniformes remplacent les premiers uniformes du régiment, qui étaient de mauvaise qualité et s'usaient vite. C2 et C3 portent les nouveaux uniformes avec leurs célèbres chemises de pompiers. Le magnifique étendard porté par l'officier survécut à la guerre mais disparut durant les années 60. Mais peu avant la mise sous presse de ce livre, on le trouva enroulé dans une boite en carton.

D Les trois Zouaves de cette planche incarnent la réputation effrayante du

Farbtafeln

A Oberst Elmer E. Ellsworth und seine United Zouave Cadets im Jahr 1860. Seltsamerweise hatte sich Ellsworth gegen die Ausstattung seiner Männer mit weit geschnittenen Hosen und einem Fes entschieden, wie es echten Zuaven entsprochen hätte, sondern seine Männer trugen stattdessen eine Uniform, die eher an die Chasseurs der französischen Armee erinnerte. Ellsworth, A1, trägt seine eigene Version der Chasseur-Uniform der Cadets, bei der ein zweireihig geknöpfter Gehrock mit roten Hosen kombiniert wird. A2 trägt auch die Chasseur-Uniform der United States Zouave Cadets, wohingegen A3 im "Zuavendress" des Regiments auftritt, der getragen wurde, wenn die Kadetten zu Exerzierübungen antraten.

B Diese beiden Zuaven der 11th New York Volunteer Infantry, den ersten Geschütz-Zuaven, tragen die erste Uniform des Regiments, die aus hellgrauen Jacken mit dunkelblauen Aufschlägen und hellgrauen Hosen besteht. Das Käppi der Figur auf Abbildung B1 trägt die Messingziffern "1FZ", die für "1st Fire Zouaves" stehen. Der Messingbuchstabe "A" gibt die Kompanie an. Die Figur auf Abbildung B2, die auf dem Bürgersteig sitzt, hat einen kahlgeschorenen Kopf, wobei ein Adler in die Stoppeln einrasiert wurde. Diese recht radikale Haartracht spiegelt wahrscheinlich den Einfluß der französischen Zuaven wider, die für ihre kahlgeschorenen Köpfe bekannt waren.

C Ein Offizier der Fire Zouaves und zwei Gefreite bei der Schlacht von First Bull Run. Der Offizier C1, der eisern die Flagge der Fire Zouaves hält, trägt einen einreihig geknöpften Gehrock, während die beiden Zuaven-Gefreiten die zweite Uniform der Fire Zouaves tragen. Diese Uniformen traten an die Stelle der ersten Uniformen des Regiments, die von schlechter Qualität und rasch abgetragen waren. C2 und C3 tragen die neue Uniform mit den berühmten Schützenhemden. Die eindrucksvolle Flagge, die vom Offizier getragen wird,

Wheat's First Special Battalion. **D1**, un Tiger Corporal, porte la veste Zouave bleue de l'unité alors que **D2** et **D3**, qui sont tous deux de simples soldats, ont abandonné leur veste et se contentent de porter une chemise rouge. Plusieurs Tigres avaient servi sous les 'Chemises Rouges' de Garibaldi avant la guerre. Comme D3, certains Tigres ne portaient pas le fez mais un chapeau de paille avec une devise patriotique sur le devant. Le célèbre pantalon rayé porté par les Tigres, dit-on, était en solide toile à matelas.

E E2 est un Charleston Zouave Cadet, membre de la compagnie des Southern Zouaves qui furent incorporés dans le South Carolina First Regiment of Rifles. Leur élégant uniforme gris gansé de rouge était coupé dans un style Chasseur. E2 est un Albany Zouave Cadet habillé avec élégance et son képi porte les lettres 'AZC' en cuivre. E2, un Caporal des Salem Zouaves, porte un uniforme de laine bleu marine avec un col gansé de cuir rouge.

F F1, un Simple soldat des Irish Zouaves, 69th New York State Militia, porte une ceinture verte et une veste de style Zouave. Le reste de son uniforme correspond à l'uniforme standard distribué au 69th New York. F1 se bat pieds nus, une habitude gaélique que certains membre du 69th New York avaient adopté à First Bull Run. Pour combattre la chaleur il a couvert son calot d'un morceau de tissu blanc nommé 'havelock'. La Figure **F2** est un simple soldat du 9th New York Volunteer Infantry, Hawkin's Zouaves, mais son pantalon est coupé plus étroit que le vrai pantalon des Zouaves. Les uniformes des Hawkins' Zouaves en surplus étaient portés par certaines unités de la milice après la guerre. La Figure **F3**, le Sergent des 10th New York, National Zouaves, porte une plaque de képi distinctive sur son turban, qui identifie son régiment.

G Parmi tous les régiments de la Guerre Civile, le 5th New York Volunteer Infantry, Duryee's Zouaves, portait l'uniforme le plus authentique. Le pantalon de F1 est coupé selon la style très bouffant et enfoncé dans ses jambières de cuir. Les autres figures de cette planche sont le Sergent John H. Berrian (**G2**) et le Sergent Andrew B. Allison (**G3**), les deux porte-étandard du 5th New York à la bataille de gains Mill, qui se détachèrent du front du 5th New York et défièrent l'ennemi. Leur uniforme porte les ganses dorées bien reconnaissables.

H H1 est un officier des Wallace's Zouaves et cette figure est inspirée d'un portrait du commandant du régiment, le Colonel Lew Wallace. La figure **H2** porte le second uniforme des Wallace's Zouaves, adopté en 1861 et que le régiment conserva jusqu'à la fin de la guerre. **H3**, un Simple soldat du 76th Pennsylvania Volunteer Infantry, les Keystone Zouaves, porte l'uniforme Zouave particulièrement attrayant de son régiment, fabriqué par l'arsenal Schuykill en Pennsylvanie.

I La figure **I1**, un Simple soldat du 72nd Pennsylvania, Baxter's Fire Zouaves, porte une veste bleu foncé gansée de rouge et un pantalon bleu ciel. La Figure Vivandière **I2** porte un 'calot de la liberté' bleu et effronté inspiré du couvre-chef que portaient les patriotes durant la Révolution Américaine. **F3**, le Sergent de Birney's Zouaves, 23rd Pennsylvania, porte une ceinture comme marque de son rang. Son képi, de modèle McClellan, est gansé de rouge.

J Les extravagants uniformes achetés en privé et portés par ces officiers du 165th New York, Second Battalion Duryee Zouaves, font paraître les uniformes standard des Zouaves bien ternes. L'illustration de l'uniforme de **J1** est basée sur la veste portée par Felix Angus, second commandant du 165th New York. Cette veste a des manches crevées jusqu'au coude et retenues par 10 boutons de cuivre. La veste portée par **J2** comporte également de riches ganses rouge et or et son képi a une bride à mousquet en position présentée. **J3**, un Simple soldat du 165th New York, monte la garde et tient son mousquet en position présentée.

K K1, un Simple soldat du 44th New York, Ellsworht's Avengers, porte un uniforme très influencé par ceux que portent les Albany Zouave Cadets. Sa chemise est particulièrement remarquable avec sa ganse bleu ciel et il porte également un pantalon de style Chasseur avec ses rayures rouges. **K2**, un Simple soldat du 140th New York Volunteer Infantry, fait partie de l'un des régiments de l'Union 'transformés' en Zouaves vers la fin de la guerre. **K3**, un Simple soldat du 146th New York Volunteer Infantry, Garrard's Tigers, porte un style d'uniforme porté par les Turcos de l'Armée Française, les troupes coloniales qui se battirent avec la même ténacité que les Zouaves.

L Le tissu de l'uniforme du 114th Pennsylvania, Collis Zouaves, que porte L1, fut importé de France durant toute la guerre. Le pantalon de style Chasseur est orné de motifs jaunes autour des poches. **L2**, la Vivandière du 114th Pennsylvania, s'inspire des images de French Mary, la plus célèbre Vivandière de la Guerre Civile Américaine. Elle porte une veste standard du 114th Pennsylvania et elle porte sa jupe par dessus un pantalon du 114th. **L3**, un Simple soldat du 155th Pennsylvania, porte un uniforme adapté des Chasseurs à pied. 10 000 de ces uniformes furent importés de France mais on se rendit compte que beaucoup d'entre eux étaient trop petits pour les Américains. Certains purent cependant être adaptés en uniformes du 155th Pennsylvania.

überlebte zwar den Krieg, ging jedoch in den 60er Jahren des zwanzigsten Jahrhunderts verloren. Kurz bevor das vorliegende Buch in Druck ging, entdeckte man sie jedoch zusammengerollt in einem Karton.

D Die drei Zuaven auf dieser Farbtafel verkörpern den Inbegriff des furchteinflößenden Rufs des Wheat's First Special Battalion. **D1**, ein Tiger Korporal, trägt die blaue Zuavenjacke der Einheit, während **D2** und **D3** - beide Gefreite - ihre Jacken abgelegt haben und nur ihre roten Hemden tragen. Vor dem Krieg hatten mehrere "Tigers" bei Garibaldis "Rothemden" Dienst getan. Wie bei D3 ersichtlich, trugen einige "Tiger" keinen Fes, sondern Strohhüte, auf deren Vorderseite patriotische Parolen zu sehen waren. Die berühmten gestreiften Hosen, die die "Tiger" trugen, wurden angeblich aus strapazierfähigem Matratzen-Drillich gemacht.

E Bei **E2** handelt es sich um einen Charleston Zouave Cadet, ein Mitglied der Kompanie von Southern Zouaves, die Teil des South Carolina First Regiment of Rifles wurden. Ihre elegante graue Uniform mit rotem Besatz war im Stil der Chasseurs geschnitten. E2 zeigt einen schick gekleideten Albany Zouave Cadet. Auf seinem Käppi sieht man das Messingzeichen "AZC". **E3** ist ein Korporal der Salem Zouaves. Er trägt eine Uniform aus dunkelblauem Wollstoff, deren Kragen mit rotem Leder eingefaßt ist.

F F1 zeigt einen Gefreiten der Irish Zouaves, 69th New York State Militia (Landesmiliz), der eine grüne Taillenschärpe und im Zuavenstil trägt. Der Rest seiner Kleidung entspricht der Standardausstattung der 69th New York. F1 kämpft barfuß, ein gälischer Brauch, dem einige Mitglieder der 69th New York bei First Bull Run Folge leisteten. Sein Käppi mit einem weißen Stoffstück, "havelock" genannt, schützt ihn vor der Hitze. Bei der Figur auf Abbildung **F2** handelt es sich um einen Gefreiten der 9th New Yorker Volunteer Infantry, Hawkins' Zouaves, seine Hosen sind jedoch enger geschnitten, als das bei echten Zuaven-Hosen der Fall war. Uniformen aus Restbeständen der Hawkins' Zouaves wurden nach dem Krieg von einigen Miliz-Einheiten getragen. Die Figur auf der Abbildung **F3**, der Feldwebel der 10th New York, National Zouaves, trägt ein charakteristisches Regimentsmützenabzeichen auf seinem Turban.

G Von allen Regimentern im Sezessionskrieg war die 5th New York Volunteer Infantry, Duryee's Zouaves, am authentischsten angezogen. Die Hosen der Figur auf F1 sind sehr weit geschnitten und in Ledergamaschen gesteckt. Bei den anderen Figuren auf dieser Farbtafel handelt es sich um Feldwebel John H. Berrian (**G2**) und den Feldwebel Andrew B. Allison (**G3**), die beiden Fahnenträger der 5th New York bei der Schlacht von Gaines Mill. Sie marschierten vor der Gefechtslinie der 5th New York und trotzten dem Feind. Ihre Uniformen zeigen den charakteristischen Gold-Besatz.

H H1 zeigt einen Offizier der Wallace's Zouaves, dessen Abbildung auf einem Porträt des Befehlshabers des Regiments, Oberst Lew Wallace, beruht. Die Figur auf der Abbildung **H2** trägt die zweite Uniform der Wallace's Zouaves, die 1861 übernommen und von diesem Regiment bis zum Kriegsende getragen wurde. **H3** zeigt einen Gefreiten der 76th Pennsylvania Volunteer Infantry, die Keystone Zouaves, der die besonders reizvolle Zuaven-Uniform des Regimentes trägt. Sie wurde vom Schuykill Arsenal in Pennsylvania gefertigt.

I Die Figur auf Abbildung **I1**, ein Gefreiter der 72nd Pennsylvania, Baxter's Fire Zouaves, trägt eine dunkelblaue Jacke mit rotem Besatz und hellblaue Hosen. Die Vivandiere-Figur auf **I2** trägt die kecke blaue "Liberty-Mütze". Die Inspiration dazu stammt von der Kopfbedeckung, die die Patrioten während der Amerikanischen Revolution trugen. **I3**, der Feldwebel der Birney's Zouaves, 23rd Pennsylvania, trägt eine Schärpe um die Taille als Zeichen seines Rangs. Sein Käppi folgt dem Muster des McClellan-Käppi und ist rot eingefaßt.

J Die aufwendigen, privat erworbenen Uniformen, wie sie diese Offiziere der 165th New York, Second Battalion Duryee Zouaves, tragen, lassen die Standarduniformen der Zuaven recht unscheinbar aussehen. Die Abbildung der Uniform von **J1** beruht auf der Jacke, die von Felix Agnus, dem zweiten Kommandeur der 165th New York, getragen wurde. Die Jackenärmel sind bis zum Ellbogen geschlitzt und mit 10 Messingknöpfen verziert. Die Jacke der Figur **J2** zeigt ebenso aufwendige rot- und goldfarbene Besätze, und sein Käppi weist einen goldfarbenen Kinnriemen auf. **J3**, ein Gefreiter der 165th New York, hat Wachdienst und trägt seine Muskete im Anschlag.

K K1, ein Gefreiter der 44th new York, Ellsworth's Avengers, trägt eine Uniform, die stark von denen der Albany Zouaves-Kadetten beeinflußt ist. Sein Hemd mit dem hellblauen Besatz ist besonders charakteristisch. Außerdem trägt er Hosen im Chasseur-Muster mit roten Streifen. **K2**, ein Gefreiter der 140th New York Volunteer Infantry, gehört einem der Regimenter der Union an, das gegen Kriegsende zu Zuaven "umgewandelt" wurde. **K3**, ein Gefreiter der 146th New York Volunteer Infantry, Gerrard's Tigers, trägt einen Uniformstil, wie man ihn von den Turcos der französischen Armee kennt, Kolonialtruppen, die genauso verwegen wie die Zuaven kämpften.

L Der Stoff für die Uniform der 114th Pennsylvania, Collis Zouaves, wie man sie bei L1 sieht, wurde den ganzen Krieg über aus Frankreich importiert. Die Hosen im Chasseur-Stil sind mit gelben Mustern um die Taschen bunt verziert. **L2**: Die 114th Pennsylvania Vivandiere beruht auf Bildern der "French Mary", der berühmtesten Vivandiere des amerikanischen Bürgerkriegs. Sie trägt die standardmäßige Jacke der 114th Pennsylvania, und ihren Rock trägt sie über einem Paar 114th-Hosen. **L3**, ein Gefreiter der 155th Pennsylvania, trägt eine umfunktionierte Uniform des Chasseur a Pied. 10.000 dieser Uniformen wurden aus Frankreich importiert, worauf man feststellen mußte, daß viele davon für die Amerikaner zu klein waren. Einige ließen sich jedoch zu Uniformen für die 155th Pennsylvania umrüsten.